BE
YOUR
BEST
BOSS

BE YOUR BEST BOSS

Reinvent Yourself from
Employee to Entrepreneur

WILLIAM R. SEAGRAVES

A PERIGEE BOOK

PERIGEE

An imprint of Penguin Random House LLC
375 Hudson Street, New York, New York 10014

Library of Congress Cataloging-in-Publication Data

Names: Seagraves, William R., author.
Title: Be your best boss : reinvent yourself from employee to entrepreneur /
    William R. Seagraves.
Description: New York : Perigee Books, 2016.
Identifiers: LCCN 2015046399 | ISBN 9780399175640 (paperback)
Subjects: LCSH: New business enterprises. | Career changes. |
    Entrepreneurship. | Self-employed. | BISAC: BUSINESS & ECONOMICS /
    Entrepreneurship. | BUSINESS & ECONOMICS / Careers / General.
Classification: LCC HD62.5 .S4195 2016 | DDC 658.1/1—dc23 LC record available at
http://lccn.loc.gov/2015046399

First edition: February 2016

PRINTED IN THE UNITED STATES OF AMERICA

1 3 5 7 9 10 8 6 4 2

Text design by Spring Hoteling

Most Perigee books are available at special quantity discounts for bulk purchases for sales promotions, premiums, fund-raising, or educational use. Special books, or book excerpts, can also be created to fit specific needs. For details, write: SpecialMarkets@ penguinrandomhouse.com.

CONTENTS

Contents

Contents

FOREWORD

Large, impersonal institutions confer degrees without wisdom; infomercials and seminars offer "coaching" that all too often is little more than a DVD set and more sales pitches.

Bill Seagraves and his wife, Theresa, are a refreshing exception to that sad norm.

The irony is, Bill's business of enabling entrepreneurs to self-fund their businesses in no way requires that they be. Bill could just as well operate like an attorney: rubber-stamping transactions, dotting i's, crossing t's, and forwarding paperwork.

Instead, Bill brings a huge added value to his financing expertise: he doesn't let his clients buy businesses they don't belong in, and he ensures that they embark on the entrepreneurial journey with eyes, ears, and sixth sense wide open.

Foreword

Having coached thousands of entrepreneurs myself as a Google AdWords consultant, I can assure you this kind of mentoring is sorely needed. Bill won't let you become his client unless you're truly qualified. He stands in contrast with thousands of biz-op salesmen whose only criteria for taking your money is that you have some to take.

That is why I'm recommending this book to you. It will take you on a journey, not only of business discovery, but also of self-discovery. Bill will explain not only the mechanics of funding your own enterprise but also how to adopt the mind-set and mental toughness that business in the twenty-first century requires.

One last word: Just like the jungle is not for domesticated pets, the entrepreneurial path is not for everyone. Many would-be entrepreneurs are merely armchair quarterbacks, living their dreams vicariously through others. They read self-help books and dream of manifesting their personal greatness but never actually do it. Others start their journey with gusto and come back in body bags.

Bill Seagraves is worthy of being your advisor. Read this book and find out if the entrepreneur's journey is truly for you.

Perry Marshall
Chicago, Illinois

Perry Marshall is the bestselling author of *Ultimate Guide to Google AdWords*, *Ultimate Guide to Facebook Advertising*, and *80/20 Sales and Marketing*.

INTRODUCTION

I always want to drive. Everyone else is welcome to be my passenger.

Even if it's just for a jaunt across town with a client or business colleague, I'm the one who whips out my car keys before anyone else can. It's always been that way. Ever since I got my driver's license, I've found a way to be the driver whenever I can. Group going to a party? I happily designate myself the sober chauffeur. Family trip and my wife offers to drive? I insist that she relax and enjoy the sights.

Even considering the hundreds of microdecisions and the risk and responsibility inherent in driving, I prefer it over being a passive passenger. Until I began writing this book, I didn't realize how much this preference carries over to my business personality.

When I used to work for other people, I was at the whim of their decisions. Even if I saw a potentially better road to take, I couldn't go there unless my boss condoned it. My employer's hands were on the wheel, not mine.

I liked corporate life in many ways, but *I could not stand this lack of control.* So in 1995 I stopped being someone's employee and became an entrepreneur, which I remain to this day.

My need to be in the driver's seat extends to money. I could not tolerate the fact that the hard-earned funds in my 401(k) were at the mercy of a volatile market. Late in 2003, during the downturn that followed the dot-com bust and the events of September 11, my wife and I began investigating nontraditional ways to invest our retirement funds. (Wall Street options were not cutting it, to say the least!)

Through readings and discussions with advisors, we learned that it was possible to invest retirement funds in your own business—without having to get in debt, without tax penalties—using a self-directed 401(k), or "rollover as business start-up," as the government calls it. I only wish I had known that eight years earlier, when I bought my first business with a seller loan!

One evening at dinner, my wife and I noted how few people in our respective business circles, our community, and among our friends and family had even heard of the self-directed 401(k). We felt lucky to have stumbled across the information, but it got us thinking, What if we made it our business to teach other entrepreneurs about this funding option?

So that's what we did. Eventually, CatchFire Funding was born. Since then, we've helped thousands of Americans who have been downsized out of a job, are afraid of being let go, or pine for the freedom of entrepreneurship for a variety of other reasons.

I know what it feels like to want that freedom and at the same time to be afraid of the unknowns involved in the leap from employee to entrepreneur.

My record hasn't been flawless. I sold one business because it ended up being the wrong long-term fit for my skills and interests. In another instance, I broke up (badly) with a business partner. And a third company stayed too long in my living room with a growing staff.

But I *learned* from all my experiences, and I was good at getting the best business advice I could afford, at striking out boldly, and at following through—all the ingredients for long-term, profitable entrepreneurship.

In the pages of this book, you'll meet dozens of new entrepreneurs from across America—former corporate warriors, public servants, or other employees who have now bought or built businesses of their own.

Their ventures range from one-person companies to businesses with a larger staff. They make products for, or supply services to, all kinds of needs in the marketplace. These once reluctant entrepreneurs range in age from their late thirties to early sixties, and they all made the leap from employee to entrepreneur midway through their careers.

You can glean lots of practical advice from these entrepreneurs' stories (and from me, as their business coach), including pros and cons, tips and tricks, and red flags. This book also offers useful checklists and worksheets. There's even a quiz to help you assess your state of entrepreneurial readiness!

As you read this book, I want you to think: What's *my* story? What makes *me* tick? What strength or passion am I overlooking or underestimating? Answer those questions, and you'll be ready to re-invent yourself and become the best boss you've ever had.

Let's get your reinvention started!

To your success.

Bill Seagraves, president
CatchFire Funding
Parker, Colorado
@catchfirefunds

PART I

Are You Ready for a New Boss?

....

Whether you're stuck in a rut at work, recently unemployed, or hanging on to your job and sanity for dear life, you have something in common with every other person who will crack the cover of this book. You have a burning desire for something more, something better, something different and new.

This burning desire—whether an ember or a full-fledged bonfire—is all you need to keep your mind open throughout this first section. I promise there will be something everyone can relate to, and that you're ready to hear it.

CHAPTER 1

....

The American Dream Gone Awry

I awoke racked with thirst, with a terrible crick in my neck and aching knees; economy class had never been kind to my six-foot-four frame. Flying high above the dark abyss of a nameless city, in who knows what time zone, I tried to picture what my wife and kids were doing while I was on the road . . . again. Soon I'd be catching up on family stories, but I wouldn't be home long enough to join in on new adventures.

But, hey, I had a source of steady income, to keep my family fed and housed and to finance some of our kids' dreams; a boss who (sort of) liked me; and I was making half-decent use of my skills and education. I was living the American dream, or at least the dream my parents raised me to believe in—or was I?

As a company man, I found I was increasingly talking myself off the ledge. My mental checklist went something like this:

Comfortable? Check.

Respected? Most of the time.

In control? Nope.

Confident about retirement? Not really.

Satisfied? Meh.

Happy . . . ?

In the grand scheme of life, weren't those last couple of things the most important? And *in control*? Ha! I felt trapped by the lifestyle I'd created for myself and my family, knowing that—at the whim of my boss or under the guise of downsizing—it could all be gone in an instant. The high-priced Silicon Valley home, private day care, a master's degree for my wife, family vacations . . .

I was certainly not holding my own hand of cards in life! Even if I stayed in the company's good graces, the best-case scenario was that in eight to ten years I could have my boss's job (which I really didn't want), and then what?

What if—I thought with real horror—I became unrecognizably removed from what I'd once set out to be?

Before I could stop it, I was flooded by memories of my impassioned words to friends, back in my college days, about the ideas and goals that excited me. There were paths I'd never taken, that I still cared about . . .

To block out these thoughts, I stuck in my earphones and frantically flicked through the radio stations on the airplane's arm rest, hoping the music would stuff down the rising lump of depression and anxiety inside me. There had to be a way out. No matter how good this career looked on the outside, I needed to find out how to make my professional life feel good *on the inside* too.

THAT SCARY TWELVE-LETTER WORD

As it turned out, my route to personal happiness and financial success was to become an entrepreneur. To many people that twelve-letter word sounds lofty and alien. But even though its linguistic roots are French, "entrepreneur" does not translate to "fear of failure" in English. In fact, "entrepreneur" was originally a workaday word that simply meant "someone who undertakes a task," or, to put it in American, someone who likes to "get 'er done."

There are all kinds of entrepreneurs out there, but what they have in common is that they don't want to work for a cold, uncaring organization but for someone who gives a damn. To that end, they realize that they themselves are the best boss they'll ever have.

GETTING THE BOOT

Maybe you've been given your marching papers after years of loyalty and hard work for a faceless corporation that's decided it no longer needs or wants you. We all know lots of people whose lives have been turned upside down since the 2008 recession.

You might be one of them; you may be feeling, for the first time in your life, like you're *disposable*. That's not a nice feeling. All of a sudden you've gone from being a smart, successful, respected professional to (cue, inner voice) a nobody, worth nothing in today's workforce.

Through the up-close-and-personal lens of your loss you may not be able to see the big picture behind your midlife career crash. And that picture is the baby boom's megademographic wave. The workplace system of yesteryear that gave tenured workers (like your parents and their parents) steady raises and good benefits, eventually providing for a comfortable retirement, is no longer sustainable. There are just too many boomers for this model to continue working.

A lucky few employees made it out of the recent recession relatively unscathed. Then there are the rest of us. And even if you did survive the gory years, you may now be watching your employer shift focus to recruiting and retaining *younger* workers.

Midcareer professionals, like yourself, are getting passed up for promotions and raises or forced into early retirement!

IT'S NOT PERSONAL

This kind of ageism exists entirely because younger people cost less to employ. In the HR column of the ledger, you've become a liability—despite being an asset with regard to experience, skills, and maturity. It's not personal—it's business. Sure, it hurts to be overlooked, but the bottom line is that the bottom line is the only benchmark that matters in the workplace.

Dan Murphy, fifty-nine, of Syracuse, New York, experienced this—on both ends. "As senior operations officer, every year I was challenged to do more with less, pushed to decrease the headcount. I pulled the trigger and did downsizing throughout my career." Then the gun got turned around and pointed at him!

"My employers felt I had gotten to a point where I was too old and too expensive," says Dan. "It was easier to pay three twentysomethings half my salary and let them work their calves off." He moved on, albeit reluctantly, and started his own business after almost two years of fruitlessly seeking a new corporate gig.

Don Rollins, sixty-two, also knows what it's like to be overlooked as "too old." When his employer merged with two other arms manufacturers—the result of government sequestering—Don learned he'd have to move to New York or the Midwest. He didn't want to leave his native Florida, so he gave up his job as director of operations, and "did what all corporate warriors do—started interviewing," he says.

It didn't go so well. "They saw my gray hair and read my résumé with my thirty years' experience . . . then I'd go to the interview, and I could feel them thinking, How much runway does this guy have left?"

Don's age turned out to be a blessing in disguise. He started his own business in Sarasota, Florida, a Signworld franchise—and he's happy he did. "I sure as hell don't miss the corporate world!" he says.

WHAT ARE YOUR OPTIONS REALLY?

Maybe you're not convinced that entrepreneurship is the answer. Maybe you're obsessing about how to fit yourself back into the corporate puzzle. (Even if it's an awkward fit, at least it's what you know.)

But the fact is, the career landscape has changed. *You've* changed—certainly in the eyes of employers.

It is highly unlikely you'll ever come across a job ad that reads like it fits you: "Seeking midlife employee with high salary demands and possibly outdated skill set. Likely to be disgruntled and in urgent need of replacement income due to family demands. Potentially overqualified and therefore likely to leave the minute something better comes along."

Julie Richter was the epitome of the disgruntled employee when she decided, at age fifty, that she could make something better come along—by herself. The Missoula, Montana, native was pretty jaded after many years as an employee in the insurance industry. "There are a lot of shenanigans and agents who only care about making the sale," she explains. "I considered getting out of the business entirely." Julie especially didn't want to work for a company anymore, "versus working for the clients, which is more important." She solved her crisis of conscience by starting her *own* insurance company, with her *own* clients to care for.

Not that it was easy. Julie admits, "I was afraid to leave a salaried, steady income and step into the unknown." She has that in common with a lot of midcareer entrepreneurs, like Dan Murphy, who says, "It was scary. I had never been self-employed. I'd always worked for large corporations. . . . Never in a million years did I think I'd start my own business!"

While Julie chose to get off the corporate train, Dan was escorted off due to downsizing. He had been managing up to 250 people at a major financial services institution, and at first he wanted back into the corporate puzzle so badly, "I was even at the point that I was willing to relocate again," he says. "But my age and income level scared new opportunities away—the same reasons for my downsizing in the first place!"

ARE YOUR GOLDEN YEARS LOSING THEIR LUSTER?

What is going to change now, or in the future, that will give you enough of an income bump to make a real difference for your retirement dreams? A series of large raises or promotions? Stock options? A lottery win?

You've been working your butt off for "the Man" for years—and who gets a new yacht or a winter home in Florida? Not you. The top executives and shareholders at your company don't need to wait until they retire to get those perks; they enjoy them now—courtesy of all your hard work.

How is your own retirement shaping up? Are you on track to get the golden years you've been dreaming of, or is the gold losing its luster?

It's possible in this day and age that you could end up being forced into early retirement by your employer. Is your nest egg big enough to cover your desired retirement?

RETIRED BUT INSPIRED

Even if you are already comfortably retired, you may be driving yourself and your spouse crazy with too much time on your hands. (After all, there are only so many things you can fix around the house!) Maybe you miss giving back to your community. Or it's possible that retirement is costing more than you anticipated, and you aren't sure how many more years of quality retirement you can afford.

In any of these cases, entrepreneurship could be an attractive option. You're not ready to be put out to pasture—physically and/or financially. You may be retired, but you're still inspired (to make a buck).

KEEPING YOUR ROOTS

It's a common scenario in this day and age of mergers and acquisitions for employees to be asked to uproot their families and relocate out of state, or even out of the United States, to accommodate a company's change in ownership. But you might be reluctant to move your spouse from a good job and your kids away from school and friends. Or maybe you don't want to be too far away from your aging parents. In any case, relocation by your employer may not be a viable solution for you.

Mike Pred, a global vice president at a leading health-care corporation, was given an ultimatum: he could relocate out of state or lose his job. He and his wife decided not to pick up and move their daughter during her high school years. Mike looked around at other work options and "concluded that I could eventually replace my income with a PrideStaff franchise while building an asset that could achieve a rate of return that would exceed what I could get in passive investments like the stock market." He made the decision to leave the corporate world in November 2013. "I have not looked back," he says.

Don Rollins faced the same kind of "relocate or you're out" choice from his corporate employer. In his case, the kids were all grown and on their own, but still Don and his wife didn't want to leave their native Florida. What Don does now, building signs for his franchise, is certainly different from being an engineer at an arms manufacturer, but, in his words, "I still get to build stuff," and he doesn't have to give up his daily contact with other people—something Don admits he just could not envision for himself, despite being, at sixty-two, close to the (old school) retirement age. Visiting customers, working alongside his employee, chatting with other local business people in the region where he lives and works—that is Don's lifeline.

IF NOT NOW, WHEN?

Even if you're still employed, you may see that you're running out of road. Your company is letting your colleagues go, one painful batch at a time, and you suspect that your number is coming up. Like a deli ticket from hell, the waiting game is as bad as, if not worse than, actually receiving the pink slip!

Maybe you're stuck in a job you no longer enjoy and you're pining for a change. You're the one who tells family and friends at each Christmas party, "This is the year I'm going to make the jump and be my own boss." And then nothing changes. Sure, change can be scary. But *feeling stuck* is worse.

Or maybe you're not looking forward to a passive retirement; many baby boomers aren't as comfortable with that as previous generations were. Dave Young, forty-nine, of Jackson, Missouri, says bluntly, "I'm not a big fan of saving your retirement funds to use when you're old, which aren't your best years." Dave is using that retirement money *now*, injecting it into his dream business (a start-up kennel and breeder).

About his own reinvention from employee to entrepreneur, Tom

Macari says, "Sometimes it's just 'put up or shut up' time!" In 2012, Tom applied for a job as police chief in Cripple Creek, Colorado, a historic gold rush town on the southwest slopes of Pikes Peak in the Rockies. He and his wife, Pattie, stayed at the area's KOA campground, and, Tom recalls, "We half-joked that if the Cripple Creek KOA ever came up for sale we should look into buying it." He didn't get the police chief job, and they went home. Then, in June 2013, the Cripple Creek KOA came on the market. It was go time for the Macaris: they put their money where their mouths were and bought the KOA business.

Even if you're younger—and nowhere near retirement—you may have had an epiphany like mine, where you realize you're not chasing the dreams of your younger self, and you can't see any good reason why not. Andrew Caplinger, thirty-five, went the corporate route for fifteen years, until he had a New Year's Eve talk with his wife, Courtney, about where he was headed. They made a pact that by a year from that date he would have launched his dream business. He followed through—and Caplinger's Fresh Catch Seafood Market was born in Indianapolis.

"I've known I've wanted to do this since I was a junior in high school," says Andrew. "We were a bunch of business dorks in the marketing club. I was part of different competitions at the national level. At one, I had to write a business plan and present it to SBA loan officers. . . . My idea was a fish market and restaurant combined. I won at the state level."

Andrew will tell you how good it feels to live up to the "boy wonder" he was twenty years before, and that all the work to become that entrepreneur has been worth it.

LIFE CHANGERS

Then there are life-changing moments that remind us how short our time is on Earth—both for us and our loved ones. These experiences can really show us what's important in life, and they may push us to embrace change *now*, rather than put it off anymore.

Pete Dailey, forty-nine, had a life-changing experience involving his father that helped him make the decision to leave his long corporate career as a meteorologist in 2014 and pursue his dream—a restaurant start-up in Oakland, California.

"Dad and I sat and talked, just the two of us, in my apartment—it was the first time we'd ever talked about me changing my career," says Pete. "Dad recommended that I do what makes me happy." A couple of weeks later, his father died suddenly in his sleep. Pete was ready to make the leap to entrepreneurship.

Or it could be your *own* mortality that gives your entrepreneurial dreams a jump start. A serious health issue had Mark Olenick reviewing his priorities and looking more closely at his next chapter. "Getting a pacemaker at age forty-three will do that," he says. Now fifty-one, Mark is going after his dream of starting a pickle company with his wife in Pennsylvania—instead of putting it off for "someday."

Life changers can also include new relationships or a point in a long-term relationship where a couple reevaluates how much time they spend together.

Michael Croteau can relate to the former situation. In his fifties, the aircraft mechanic wanted to find a job where he could work closely with his fiancée, Tina. So he left his career with a large aeronautical corporation and bought an existing business back east, where he grew up—a quaint vacation resort in the heart of the New Hampshire Lakes Region. "I wanted something that would support us and something that we could do *together*," says Michael.

VELVET SHACKLES

If you are still working for someone else, take a moment to consider how the next decade will likely play out. Do you think you'll have control over how and when your career ends? Will you even get a *say* in the matter? You could be wearing velvet shackles that look good and feel comfortable now—but shackles are still shackles.

Michael Schaul, fifty-seven, knows about shackles, and how they can creep up on you despite your best intentions or how happily your career started.

Michael spent the first decade of his career with a large US oil company at its small offices in Africa, China, and other international spots. He loved the hands-on work he did there. "In my mind, I made more powerful decisions overseas," he says.

When Michael and his wife moved back to Chicago to start a family, he found the large corporate culture there didn't offer "as much job satisfaction for me." He missed being able to make fast decisions as a country manager who "didn't have to go up three layers of management for approval." So despite better pay and great exposure, he left corporate America and started consulting for a couple of years ("loved the work, hated the travel"), then bought an apparel company in Wisconsin. So began Michael's satisfying twenty-year entrepreneurial journey.

Layers of management and the "analysis paralysis" of the boardroom-meeting culture are shackles that former corporate warrior Mike Pred does not miss. He says he and his employees at his PrideStaff franchise in Lilburn, Georgia, "can focus our efforts on what we determine to be the most valuable—and eliminate the cumbersome elements of decision making in the corporate world." Mike adds that as an entrepreneur, "There are no excuses, no finger pointing, and no politics. . . . I know that the results of my business totally hinge on my effort and the team I put in place."

Amy Shellart is clear about why she launched her own business, the Goodness Locker Inc., in Springfield, Missouri. "I need to be in charge of my own destiny. . . . If I piss off my boss, I can't provide for my family," says the forty-one-year-old who is raising two preteen kids with her life and business partner, Christina Hesse.

Whether you're motivated by inspiration or desperation, whether you are pursuing a dream or adapting to the changing workplace—shaking off the shackles is worth the effort. And here's some more good news: you're likely in a much better position to become an entrepreneur than you think!

THE LEGIONS OF "YEAH, BUTS"

Sometimes entrepreneurs start out with a bunch of "yeah, buts" that explain why they can't, or shouldn't, start their own business. These may sound familiar.

"Yeah, but I don't have time to start over with a new career, not at my age!"

Here's the thing, though: you're not starting over! It's not at all like coming out of college. You're bringing with you a whack of real-world experience, maturity, people skills, money management skills, and more. A move to entrepreneurship at a later stage in life is more like a transition, a reinvention, than a start-up.

Dan Murphy knows this because in the business he bought, he handles all the sales and marketing (he's a common sight in his region, driving his branded SUV), as well as bookkeeping. His college education in finance plus three decades working in the banking industry have been a huge asset, as has all that time working with other people. (Let's see a twentysomething bring all that to the party!)

"Yeah, but I don't know anything about entrepreneurship— I don't even know what I don't know!"

It's true, you may lack exact knowledge of what knowledge you're lacking, but relax—you can get up to speed pretty quickly. Because you're mature, have made years' worth of big decisions, and have good people skills, you won't have any problem

- researching all the options out there,

- seeking out conversations with entrepreneurs who have ventures similar to what you're considering,

- surrounding yourself with experienced professional (such as financial and legal) advisors,

- and weeding out misinformation by running it past those trusted advisors.

"Yeah, but I don't have the money to finance my own business. I have bills to pay and kids to put through college!"

Finding the funding for your new business is a serious hurdle, but there are more ways around it than you think. Debt is not your only option! There are options such as self-directed retirement funds (without tax or penalty). Many people are holding on to their retirement funds, whether in a 401(k) or IRA, because, frankly, they just don't know that those funds can be rolled over into a new business.

"Yeah, but don't half of all new businesses fail?"

Starting a business is hard work but, then again, so are most worthwhile things in life. How easy is raising kids? How easy is it to stay happily married long term? You know the odds of matrimony failing, but that doesn't stop you from giving it a try!

Besides, failure is not really an option if you do your research and due diligence, invest wisely, and give your new business 100 percent of your effort.

If you focus on other people's failures, how can you emulate other people's successes? Stick with the winners. Avoid the losers.

David Coleman knows about fear of failure. The corporate man turned owner of USA Auto Glass of Naples, Florida, says it can be frightening to start a business, "because now you're responsible for your own self and, in many cases, employees too. But, by the same token, if you're one of those employees, you're going to be *stuck in that hamster wheel* for the rest of your life."

He adds, "The initial work [as a business owner] transforms itself further down the road into a lifestyle that most people can't imagine. It just makes it so much easier once you attain that level—it *becomes enjoyable again to go to work!*"

Don Rollins, the sixtysomething Signworld franchise owner, says that "Being an entrepreneur is not a lazy man's deal. . . . It's a whole lot different than back when I had a staff to delegate work to." But he adds that now all his hard work directly benefits *him*, and not some employer: "It's my money. It's my deal. I can make decisions as *I* see fit."

"Yeah, but everyone says I don't have what it takes to be an entrepreneur!"

We've all, at some time in life, found ourselves at the end of other people's "head trash"—the sort of knee-jerk negative reactions family, friends, coworkers, even strangers, can have to an idea they aren't familiar with. Sadly, this head trash will likely appear when you start talking about entrepreneurship and how you're going to do it.

Joseph Davern, owner of Davern's Tavern & Lounge in Justice, Illinois, knows the feeling. Soon after he learned about the self-directed 401(k) funding option, Joseph says, he dealt with serious skepticism from family members, namely his brother, who was a vice president of a large company. "He was convinced that the transaction was impossible," recalls Joseph. After a few more talks with CatchFire Funding, Joseph's brother "actually got on board." Joseph didn't let a beloved sibling's doubt deter him from pursuing entrepreneurship.

When Mark and Tracey Olenick, of Venango, Pennsylvania,

started their pickle business from scratch while raising four young children, Mark left behind a twenty-year corporate career. "Everyone had lots of opinions on what we should do," Mark recalls. For example, Tracey's father said, "*I would never do it, but if anyone can, it's you two.*" That's a nice touch from Dad, throwing in his vote of confidence while sharing his own fear of entrepreneurship.

Naysayers will always exist in the world, and most of them don't mind weighing in! But here's a critical tip: do not seek validation from people with *no entrepreneurial experience.* Their concerns could be well-meaning, but they aren't backed up with credibility. It is not your job to convince everyone else that you're making a good decision. (Convincing your spouse and your bank is another story!)

"Yeah, but I don't want to lose the friends I've made at work."

Maybe you're worried about your professional social life. If you have a network of colleagues and friends you spend time with at the office, and sometimes even during off-hours, will life as an entrepreneur be lonely?

It might be—at least at first. The corporate world and the entrepreneur/business-owner community rarely overlap. Moving from one to the other can be a difficult adjustment, but it's up to you to build a new network of friends and colleagues you can trust. (Of course, your family and nonwork friends aren't going anywhere, regardless of the type of employment you choose.)

As Peter Dailey, who became a new entrepreneur in Oakland, California, after decades as a career meteorologist, says, "I may miss the people, the friends I made at work, but I sure don't miss the cutthroat corporate world!"

"Yeah, but what I really love to do won't make a viable business."
You'd be surprised. You may have heard the expression, "You tend to be good at what you love doing." Well, it generally holds true that if you start a business based in something you're passionate about—and you have the skills and there's a market demand, of course—you'll be successful. It just makes sense. We get good at what we do over and over, by choice, and often that begins as a hobby or side occupation. Adore going to dog shows? Have you looked into how many breeders or kennels there are in your area? Always been a computer nerd? Look into running a computer-repair service. You get the idea. So go for it!

CHAPTER 2

···

Don't Sell Yourself Short

YOU COULD BE READIER THAN YOU THINK

You may be selling yourself short when it comes to how prepared you
think you are to become an entrepreneur. You've likely accumulated a
lot of technical and people skills, as well as project, budget management, communications, and teamwork experience—all of which puts
you in a great position for running your own business.

Corporate life "is a paid college education," says Andrew Caplinger, who worked for fifteen years in positions such as seafood buyer
and assistant floor manager at a major chain before starting his own
fish market in 2013. He learned good management practices on his
employer's dime—lessons that have proven vital for all the hats he
now wears as owner of Caplinger's Fresh Catch Seafood Market in his
hometown of Indianapolis.

Mark Olenick says he transferred skills—such as learning concepts and developing work teams—from his nineteen years as a project manager at a large investment-management company, to his new entrepreneurial venture, Luke's Cukes, where he only manages family members but juggles retail, food service, manufacturing, sales, marketing, renovations/expansions, and soon a new diversified line of business.

Like Andrew, Mark, and other midlife entrepreneurs, you've learned a lot more at your corporate job than you may realize, including

- how to manage finances, create a budget, and meet targets;

- how to manage projects with lots of moving parts and players;

- how to grow a thick skin to handle criticism and ups and downs;

- and how to play well with others in forming and being part of teams.

Youth (a surplus of energy and time) is wasted on the young! But wisdom—well, it and the skills you've accrued over the decades—is great fuel for midcareer entrepreneurship.

Age is, in fact, a *real advantage* for entrepreneurship. Consider that if you are forty-five or older,

- you entered the workforce when there was no Internet, there were no mobile phones, and maybe not even computers in the office (no shortcuts in the old school of hard knocks!);

- you aren't as likely to sweat the small stuff; as a mature person you've outgrown drama and have developed a realistic, long-term view of work;

- and you've become an independent thinker—you've learned you can trust yourself to make hard decisions.

YOU KNOW HOW TO PLAY NICE WITH OTHERS

In a typical corporate setting, not enough value is placed on what you learn about human nature, including your own nature. I mean insights such as that you don't know everything in the world, or that you attract a lot more with honey than with vinegar, and skills like how to work with people who are completely different from you—and much more.

People skills don't come easily—especially if you happen to be an introvert. However, working in a corporate setting for many years tends to beat the shyness out of you, shaping you into someone who's comfortable dealing with new people and situations. Aside from the traditional writer—locked alone in his or her tower all day, every day, birthing words—pretty much every job requires people skills.

YOU MIGHT BE SMARTER THAN YOUR BOSS

Before becoming an entrepreneur, Felix Garcia, fifty-four, of Albuquerque, New Mexico, was feeling frustrated with the stranglehold of dysfunction that chokes the public sector. "Most people don't know systems or process improvement. . . . They don't know how to set goals or run meetings effectively," says Felix, who spent twenty years as a high school teacher and university administrator.

A proponent of lifelong learning, Felix is working on his third degree—this one in industrial organizational psychology, from the University of New Mexico (he already holds degrees in special education and education administration). Felix wanted to take his knowledge and aptitude and apply it somewhere where he could see real results—and *control* those results. The more he looked into entrepreneurial options, the more he felt renewed passion for business improvements and gained a new perspective on his motivations.

Like Felix, you may recognize that you are smarter than your boss or bosses. And when you know you can do better, it's agonizing to squirm in your chair, year after year, powerless to change an organization.

So Felix walked away from his career as a public servant and started his own business-coaching business. His wife Vicki, fifty-one, has supported his entrepreneurial venture, which began shortly after the youngest of their five children left for college. "Before it had always been about the kids," says Vicki. "Now it's *our* time!"

Speaking of kids . . .

YOU SERVE AS A ROLE MODEL

At this place in your life, you may have dependents or other family members who look up to you, and you may wish to serve as a role model for personal empowerment, for overcoming fear and other obstacles and taking control of one's life.

Felix and Vicki Garcia wanted to leave a legacy for their children—not just money created by the business, but lessons on how "to improve their lives . . . even if just by exposing them to another world—a world of self-reliance they may not have considered before," says Felix.

Amy Shellart and her partner, Christina Hesse, involve their two preteens in the healthy-vending-machine company they started. They feel very proud that their kids help with taste testing and shopping for food and drinks for the machines. The kids even helped come up with the name, the Goodness Locker Inc.

Julie Richter, with three children and five granddaughters, knows about legacies and role models. She hired her daughter, Tabitha, to work as her mobile administrative assistant and is now hiring her brother, a retired teacher, as an independent contractor (agent) with her company, Compass Insurance Group, in Missoula, Montana. After all, says Julie, "It's the American dream, for people to be their own boss!"

What are you teaching *your* children—whatever age they are—about making their own way in today's working world?

YOU'VE GOT THE SKIN OF A RHINO

Wisdom also comes in the form of a tough skin. After decades of learning not to take work too personally (what your boss or coworkers say, what decisions get made at executive level, etc.), you're practically a rhino. A tough hide will prove invaluable as you enter the world of entrepreneurship, where your ego is on the line a lot of the time.

As we age, we also realize that the only constant is change, and that few changes are catastrophic. We adapt, develop a backbone and the stamina to get through life's unexpected hurdles, and we come to appreciate how much work is needed for success.

For example, after a dozen years running her own day spa, Julie Richter developed allergies to many of the hair- and body-care products she worked with. She also suffered chronic back and foot pain from standing all day at the salon. Around the same time, her first marriage broke up, and she moved, with three kids, back to her hometown in Montana. Today she owns a successful insurance company, has remarried, and spends time with her five granddaughters whenever she can.

Let's see a young "trep" (twentysomething slang for "entrepreneur") show that kind of resilience and adaptability! Overcoming adversity and juggling many professional and personal priorities over a period of decades is experience that can really pay off for an entrepreneur.

YOU'VE PRACTICED MAKING MONEY

At some point in your career you've likely had to balance a budget for a project, department, or division. The higher up you get, the bigger the budgets; you may even have been managing millions of dollars.

However, when you become an entrepreneur, and it is now your *own* money you're managing, you may find accounting scarier than you did in your corporate life.

But really it shouldn't be any different: the rules of accounting or economics don't change just because you're the owner. You still need to account for every dollar spent, to see that it's correctly allocated and accounted for every quarter and at the end of every year—just as when you worked for someone else.

The number one skill behind entrepreneurial success is to *practice making money*. Like every skill in life, you need to practice, practice, practice to get good at it. Don't be afraid to make mistakes; you learn from them and will just get stronger at money management.

RETIREMENT FUNDS CAN WORK FOR YOU *NOW*

As mentioned, a big advantage often overlooked by midcareer wannabe entrepreneurs—often because they've never heard of it—is self-directed 401(k) or IRA funds being rolled over into their own corporations. Or maybe they've heard of it but are skeptical about its legality and tax implications.

If you don't at least *look* into the self-directed 401(k), you're missing out. Tapping into your retirement funds puts you in the enviable position of starting a business with *positive cash flow* and thus with no looming pile of debt hovering above your head. It's the kind of cash infusion that is critical to running a sustainable business, especially if you're getting a later start as an entrepreneur.

Tom and Pattie Macari funded their purchase of the Cripple Creek campgrounds with a self-directed 401(k), to help them avoid tax penalties. At first, though, they were reluctant, being concerned about the legality of it all. After consulting with experts, and discovering that it's all aboveboard, says Tom, "We were able to fund our business through the purchase of stock in our own business, using our 401(k) money."

Dave Petty, fifty, launched Double Rafter D Enterprises Inc., in Chelsea, Oklahoma, entirely without debt—through the rollover of his substantial 401(k), which he'd accrued over decades as an oil industry executive, into his own corporation. "I worked awful hard to accumulate what I had and didn't want to lose it," says Dave. "I'm also confident in the business we're doing, that we can make more money each year than in the stock market. . . . I plan on living another twenty-five, thirty years, and I want my money to still be there." He and his wife, Dawn, worked together on their start-up, a business that provides video-recording and instant-replay electronic-scoreboard services to professional rodeos across the United States.

Michael Croteau and his fiancée, Tina, used his 401(k) funds, accrued during long-time employment in the aeronautics industry, to deal with *unexpected costs* after buying a business. A month after they took over a rural New Hampshire hotel, its water main burst, flooding everything, and the main house had to be rid of asbestos. Because Michael was able to roll over the money from his 401(k) to fund the business—without taxes or early withdrawal penalties—he had a built-in cushion, which would not likely have been the case if he'd had to get a traditional business loan.

In fact, when Michael was considering whether the self-directed 401(k) funding vehicle was right for him and his situation, he had to take an especially important factor into account—the seasonal nature of the cottage-rental business on the East Coast. Having taken over the business in late summer, the Croteaus were concerned about how they would survive the upcoming winter months with no income.

"With the rollover process, I was able to set aside some money to make sure we got through the first winter," says Michael. "Until we knew what kind of income the business could generate, this 'safety net' made a huge difference." What's more, the couple was able to use some of the rollover money to upgrade the cottages with new mattresses and kitchen appliances.

YOUR PASSION CAN TURN INTO CASH

The Pettys are a good example of turning passion into a viable business opportunity. Dawn's face lights up as she watches her husband talk about rodeo. "We live our passion every day, every week," she says. Dave adds, "There's nothing like owning your own business, no matter what that business is, especially when it's successful—it's one of the greatest feelings in the world."

Can you imagine how you'd feel if you were doing something that ignited a fire inside you every day?

You may not think the particular skills you've picked up over the years, and the passions you've nurtured, are all that special. Maybe you bake exquisite pastries, are a genius at small-engine repair, love to work on taxes, or have a real concern about health trends. If you see your passions as mere hobbies, you could be missing the boat—these interests might be your ticket to an encore career!

Mark Olenick, the artisan-pickle maverick of Pennsylvania, looks back on the first half of his life and reflects, "My true love is food. If I had it to do again, I would have pursued a culinary career." He grew up learning about the artisan craft of fermentation at the knee of his father who, in turn, had learned it from his father. For years, Mark and his wife, Tracey, pickled products at home for their family and friends. An ever-growing fan base finally convinced them to start selling the goods.

Food was also the first love of Pete Dailey, who had a long and profitable career predicting the weather in major cities across the United States. He left it all behind to start a restaurant business, Homemade Oakland. This California eatery serves crowdsourced family recipes adapted by local culinary school students. "Science and food have always been my twin passions. . . . When I applied to get a PhD in meteorology at UCLA, I applied to the Cordon Bleu chef school at the same time," says Pete.

Amy Shellart, of Springfield, Missouri, followed her passion for healthy eating right into a great business idea and a start-up. She has worked in chronic-disease management for years, mostly in the design and maintenance of diabetes programs. "So many people with diabetes are overweight; they have poor eating habits," says Amy who, at forty-one, started eating healthier and working out at the gym. "I had to walk by a vending machine with Coke, sticky buns, chocolate bars, to get to the fitness machines. . . . Same thing with hospitals—bad vending! Where are you supposed to get healthy foods?" That passion—coupled with an underserved space in the market—merged in the development of her business idea, placing natural-food vending machines in her community.

Which passion of *yours* could you turn into a viable business?

HIGHER EDUCATION ISN'T A PREREQUISITE

Dave Young, of Jackson, Missouri, may have ceased his formal studies after high school graduation, but his career in the military and in corporate IT and sales (when he managed up to sixty employees) stood him in good stead when it came to starting his own business.

"I've always been self-taught. I have a get-it-done attitude," says Dave, forty-four, a single dad of three grown sons and now the owner of Sweet Pea Kennels. "When I was traveling for sales in my career, I would visit local kennels across the country to see how they do business. I'm always crunching numbers . . . thinking about how to pay less to the tax man, how to build without debt, how to expand in the most efficient manner."

Julie Richter, who now owns her own insurance company, never questioned if she had what it takes to be an entrepreneur. Besides studying cosmetology in her early twenties, she says her education has been "self-training—personal growth, webinars, and seminars in small business, in personal growth . . . I think that's essential to all entrepreneurs."

Dave and Julie are among many entrepreneurs who are successful despite not having a formal education in business, or other higher learning; they have the goods in skills, experience, work ethic, tenacity, and passion.

By now, you're probably convinced that you've been selling yourself short when it comes to what you might bring to the entrepreneurial party.

Now let's go a bit deeper. Grab a pen, maybe your life partner or spouse, and get ready for some self-assessment of how your personality may lend itself to entrepreneurship.

CHAPTER 3

....

How Entrepreneurially Ready Are You?

EVALUATE YOUR ENTREPRENEURIAL READINESS

You don't have to be an Oprah Winfrey fan to understand the value of self-awareness, and as someone likely in your late forties or older, you've had lots of chances to get to know yourself. But that doesn't necessarily mean you know yourself as an *entrepreneur*.

The Small Business Administration (SBA) defines "entrepreneur" as "a person who organizes and manages a business undertaking, assuming the risk for the sake of profit."

That definition is telling in a few ways:

a.   "Who *organizes and manages*" indicates a level of operational experience that, quite frankly, only comes with age.

b. "Assuming the *risk*" emphasizes the fact that it takes being comfortable with uncertainty to be a successful entrepreneur.

c. "For the sake of *profit*" shows a commitment to the practice of making money.

The following short quiz will help you assess your entrepreneurial readiness—i.e., how well you embody those three simple qualities we just extracted from the SBA definition of "entrepreneur."

It's a good idea to involve your spouse or life partner, either by taking the quiz together or discussing your results afterward.

Respond to each question with the *first honest answer that comes to you.* Ready? Assess your entrepreneurial readiness!

1. IF I WAS LEFT ALONE ON A DESERTED ISLAND, I WOULD

a. probably go insane from loneliness.

b. eventually adapt to the situation.

c. be as happy as a clam.

2. THE MOST MONEY I'VE RISKED IN EITHER A BUSINESS VENTURE, GAMBLING, OR OTHER SITUATION IS

a. a month's wages.

b. a year's wages.

c. more than a year's wages.

3. WHEN A VENTURE DIDN'T PAY OFF FOR ME, I FELT

a. devastated; I'll never do it again.

b. down for a week or so, then I bounced back.

c. nothing ventured, nothing gained . . . on to the next venture!

4. WHEN I HAVE TO MAKE AN IMPORTANT BUSINESS DECISION, I FEEL

a. analysis paralysis; I seek someone else to make the decision.

b. some anxiety and procrastination, but I follow through.

c. energized and fully engaged.

5. WHEN THINKING OF INVESTING, I EXPECT A RETURN ON MY INVESTMENT

a. as soon as possible (i.e., within the first year).

b. in the short term (over the next couple of years).

c. over a longer term (five or more years).

6. WHEN I WORK IN A TEAM, WHAT I REALLY WANT TO DO IS

a. stay quiet so I don't cause conflict.

b. build consensus so everyone gets heard.

c. take the lead, have control.

7. I WOULD PREFER TO BE INVOLVED IN A TEAM SPORT AS

a. a spectator.

b. a coach, trainer, or helper.

c. a key player on the team.

8. IF I IMAGINE HAVING A BUSINESS EMPIRE IN THE FUTURE, I FEEL

a. skeptical; it's not likely to happen.

b. cautiously optimistic about the possibility.

c. gung ho—let's get 'er done!

Now add up your points:

1 point for each *a* answer

2 points for each *b* answer

3 points for each *c* answer

If your total number of points is

8: You're probably not ready to be an entrepreneur at this time in your life. But don't give up; do some more soul-searching and research, and take this quiz again in a few months or a year.

9–16: You're ready to become your own boss, cautiously at first. A "Company of One," such as buying a franchise, might be a good start for you at this time.

17–23: You're busting to get started! Your best options probably fall under the "Boss of a Few" or "Business of Many" headings—that is, either buying an existing business or franchise, or creating a start-up.

24: Wow! You're slated to become an entrepreneur on steroids—growing your venture quickly via diversification or multiple units.

To take a more in-depth version of this entrepreneurial readiness quiz, go to yourbestboss.com/quiz.

PART II
Size Matters!

....

Congratulations, you have what it takes to be an entrepreneur and open the door to an exciting new world of opportunity! Actually, a whole set of *different* doors. You'll be glad to learn that entrepreneurship offers a plethora of options . . . and decisions: such as figuring out what size and type of business to start at this point in your life.

Size matters: you need to find a business opportunity that's just the right fit—one that takes into account your level of investment, taste for control and risk, people skills, and desired rate of growth.

Start a venture that's too small and you might outgrow it quickly. Start too big and you could find the business difficult to manage effectively, or you might end up struggling with cash-flow problems.

In this section, we'll discuss your options when it comes to the size of your new business and how you might make your venture *scalable* (i.e., expandable), to move you up the next rung of the entrepreneurial ladder.

CHAPTER 4

Company of One

The first, and simplest, way to become a "Company of One" is to be a consultant—to do the kind of work you do in your career, only as your own boss, not someone's employee. I became an independent consultant for a year after I left corporate employment, but I realized quickly that I needed a more scalable business plan if I was going to make the income I wanted and needed.

The Company of One comes in many forms beyond a consulting business. It might be an HVAC, handyman, or computer service; doing plumbing, graphic design, web development, interior decorating, or garage and closet organization; making window coverings; being a personal chef; or serving as an insurance or financial advisor. Many other lines of business, too, can be run by a single person.

For some entrepreneurs, running a Company of One is a soul-searching phase, a time to answer key questions: Who do I really want to be as my own boss? Who am I passionate about serving? Which of my abilities am I most confident about? How much do I really like managing people?

The Company of One model can be a long-term plan or a short-term bridge to the "Boss of a Few" model or founding a "Business of Many" down the road. (That's the beauty of entrepreneurship—you never have to stop growing and improving!)

WHY A COMPANY OF ONE COULD BE A GOOD FIT FOR YOU

The Company of One model of entrepreneurship could be a good fit for you, especially if

- you want to keep it simple and are seeking a relatively straightforward business, at least for now;

- you like to do things a certain way—namely, your way—and involving other people could mean compromises you aren't willing to make, at least not at the start of your entrepreneurial journey;

- you're looking for a change from managing people, something you've done for years in your career, and "solopreneuring" sounds very appealing to you;

- you aren't on the high end of the risk-taking spectrum, and even if it means your return on investment is lower, you'd rather play it on the safe side.

YOUR OPTIONS AS A COMPANY OF ONE
Man in a Van

One popular form of one-person franchising is the "man in a van" model—an affectionate term for a franchisee whose office is his or her vehicle. This can be a very cost-efficient way to get started—no need for the upfront brick-and-mortar investment required for a retail, food service, office, or production space.

Dan Murphy is a man in a van. He drives around Syracuse, New York, in his SUV, which is vinyl wrapped in signage for the CertaPro Painters franchise he bought. Dan does sales, marketing, bookkeeping— all the work for his Company of One, except the actual painting. (He hires local crews for that.)

After being downsized out of his management job at a large financial-services corporation, Dan was sitting at home, wondering what his next step would be, when he got a call from a franchise recruiter who found him via an online network.

"Before, if anybody had reached out to me about any opportunity except for corporate work, I would have gotten off the phone as quickly as possible," admits Dan. However, forced by circumstances to keep an open mind, he ended up buying a license for the painting franchise and is now more than breaking even after a challenging first two years in business.

Home Based

Obviously, working at home can keep down the costs of your Company of One—no need to lease a space. However, you should be sure your state's laws permit you to have a home-based business. For example, when Julie Richter started her insurance business in Missouri, she was required to rent a small office space to receive couriers and other types of business deliveries.

I've worked out of my home more than once: first, during my short-lived gig as an engineering consultant (my first foray into entrepreneurship), and then, many years (and a few businesses) later, when I crowded my family home with a growing number of CatchFire Funding employees—that is, until my wife put her foot down (rightly so) and we found an office to lease.

One-Person Start-Up

The smaller scale of the Company of One business model allows you to take an idea, add your skills, and get it on the market in a relatively short period of time.

That was the case with the niche service Dave and Dawn Petty started for the rodeo profession. The couple works out of their truck and trailer, and "Every day we are on the road, from Louisiana to Montana, visiting our rodeo family," says Dawn. (The Pettys are the only employees, and as a couple, they can still be classified as a Company of One.) Because the Pettys knew the rodeo business well and had a straightforward service in mind for their start-up—renting video recording equipment and big screens to rodeos—they found getting the business going a relatively nimble process.

Likewise, Julie Richter knew her industry well before she jumped to solopreneurship. Her years selling insurance for an employer, and the relationships she had developed there, eased her way in starting up her company, Compass Insurance Group. Thanks to her connections and reputation, Julie went from having zero clients ("I didn't buy a book of business") to about one hundred clients in her first seven months of business—unusual in the insurance industry, where, she says, "It's very hard to convince insurance companies to trust a new independent broker to sell their products."

It's a Family Affair

A Company of One can include a business in which the only employees are family members. Such is the case with Dave Young, whose grown sons are working for his kennel business. It's also a family affair for the Olenicks, the Pennsylvania pickle dynasty. They haven't yet hired any employees for Luke's Cukes—all the work is done by the couple and their teenage daughter and son.

One-Person Existing Business

Purchasing a preexisting Company of One is trickier and less common. This is because a one-person operation relies, by its very nature, on the skills and relationships of its owner/operator. There is considerable risk of customers leaving when the owner does. Also, the smaller scale of the Company of One means you are not likely to get many (if any) assets in the sale.

However, it can work to buy an existing one-person business *if* together with the business you are buying a strong customer list in a highly commoditized industry—such as an established neighborhood pest-control service. In the case of an insurance or other financial services Company of One, you could be buying "a book of business," meaning you will take over its existing accounts.

PROS OF THE COMPANY OF ONE
Lighter Investment

A Company of One needs less start-up capital. Having no employees means less (or no) overhead for office space, no salaries (other than your own) or benefits or training, nor any need for payroll accounting or HR management.

More Control

If it's just you—no partner, no employees, no head office, no investors—you get to call all the shots. There are no office politics to negotiate, no compromises to make. This kind of complete control may be the single most important aspect to you in starting a business. If so, you're in the right place with a Company of One: you don't have anyone to answer to except yourself (and perhaps your spouse).

Pursue Your Passion

The small scale afforded by the Company of One model gives you all the flexibility in the world, so you are free to pursue your passion and translate it into a profitable business. What have you always wanted to do that your career never gave you the time or the freedom to pursue?

CONS OF THE COMPANY OF ONE
Expansion Is Elusive

In the course of business ownership, there will come a time—maybe sooner, maybe later—when you will wish you could clone yourself!

Once your business begins to experience success, you are likely to hit a ceiling in growth and return on investment if you have no employees.

Unstructured

It can be tempting not to bother with formal structures when you start a Company of One, but that would be a mistake. You should follow the same "best practices" that work for any other size company—whether you franchise, buy an existing business, or create a start-up. For example, legally incorporate your Company of One so at the very least you can write off all your work-travel and meal expenses, supplies, etc.

Loneliness

If you're coming out of the corporate world, where you were surrounded by people all the time, you'll likely run smack into loneliness, which can become the bane of the Company of One. If you're an extreme extrovert, you should give this business model some serious second thought. Working alone takes a certain type of person, and it's okay if you're not that type. Just know ahead of time that that's who you are. (Your answers to the entrepreneurial readiness quiz in chapter 3 will help you identify this.)

Is That All There Is?

Boredom can creep into your Company of One if you don't keep it fresh—new quotas, new customers, new products and/or services, new markets, etc. Even if you're fine with having no coworkers, you are going to want stimulating work. After all, boredom is often a reason why many people opt out of the corporate rat race!

COMPANY OF ONE CHECKLIST

❑ List everything you're good at and care about (yes, even hobbies) to see what might provide long-term satisfaction for your new business.

❑ Figure out what level of investment you can bring to your venture initially.

❑ Try to figure out how working alone might suit you. Talk to your friends, spouse, and other family about how *they* think you'd do as a solopreneur.

❑ Incorporate your new business right out of the gate. Becoming You Inc. or You LLC has great benefits in tax write-offs.

❑ Don't overlook the support of family members as (unpaid) employees, at least at the start, or as helpers in other parts of your life, so you can devote yourself to your Company of One.

CHAPTER 5

···

Boss of a Few

The "Boss of a Few" business model is the next rung up the entre-preneurial ladder in terms of number of employees (one to five), amount of up-front investment, and relative risk. As boss of a few, your return on investment can be larger, and quicker, than with a Company of One, so some midcareer entrepreneurs prefer to start with this model.

WHY BOSS OF A FEW COULD BE A GOOD FIT FOR YOU

The Boss of a Few model may be a good place to start if the following description fits you:

- You don't view yourself as a major risk taker, yet you're also not completely risk averse.

- You're pretty good at weighing your options but are generally quick to act when a good opportunity presents itself.

- You are comfortable collaborating with people and believe that more heads are better than one.

My own journey illustrates the Boss of a Few model. After I left my corporate gig, I began researching business opportunities. Given my engineering background, I thought something in the computer world would be interesting. I worked with three brokers, who walked me through a mix of franchises and existing businesses for sale. I weighed my options and became the proud owner of an on-site computer-repair and network-services business in the Denver area.

With that business, I inherited three employees: two service techs and one person who took calls and scheduled appointments. I took one or two service calls a day myself. Overall, it was a pretty well-run operation, so there was nothing to do in the way of restructuring, at least initially.

About six months in, I saw that my techs were getting hired away by some of my bigger clients, who wanted to have in-house computer experts on staff. To replace them, I began hiring local graduates of a ten-week technical-training course. Then the Y2K phenomenon hit—the widespread fear that the clock change to the year 2000 would mess up computers. My business could barely keep up with the demand, and our "quick-response" service made scheduling more difficult. I increased my employee count to eight, the highest it would ever go.

When the Y2K crisis settled down, I had to lay off each of the techs I'd hired until, a year later, it was down to me and John, an employee who'd been with me since almost the beginning. A couple of years later, John and I arranged for him to buy me out.

To be honest, there was more to my exit from this Boss of a Few business. I'd discovered I didn't like crawling around in the dust under people's desks, with wires hanging in my face, and that I wasn't making the best use of my skills and interests. However, those eight years as the boss of a few were a wonderful learning experience, and they helped me immeasurably in my next level of entrepreneurship.

STAFF WITH THE RIGHT STUFF

Smart staffing is particularly vital to the Boss of a Few model. That's because with such a lean workforce you need to be sure that every worker is the absolute best fit for his or her role. The rule "hire slowly, fire fast" is a good one to follow when it comes to successful staffing.

Sometimes you have to make hard decisions to keep on track with your goals, especially if you only have one employee. Such was the case with Don Rollins when he left the corporate arena and bought a Signworld franchise.

In his first nine months of running Great Blue Images, Don slightly more than broke even, which he considers quite an accomplishment given, as he says, that he "wasted about half that time with the wrong employee." Don eventually replaced that worker with an "extraordinarily talented millennial guy. . . . Together we are building a following." Now he'd like to expand his twenty-five-hundred-square-foot facility, add a CNC (computerized numerical control) machine, and hire a few more "right fit" employees.

EXPERIENCE NOT REQUIRED (BUT IT DOESN'T HURT)

Launching a Boss of a Few business is obviously easier if you've had some experience managing people and/or running your own business in the past. If you've done so, don't overlook this as a real asset to your success and perhaps a reason to jump straight to the Boss of a Few model.

Dave and Pattie Christianson didn't know each other when they ran small businesses early in their careers. Dave had developed steam-cleaning and health-product-distribution businesses, all while keeping his full-time job as a project manager in the defense industry and getting a degree in IT at night school. Pattie had started a day spa, had retail-management experience, and had helped her ex-husband start a business selling cold drinks to tourists in Santa Fe.

Pattie and Dave, now fifty-two and fifty-one, respectively, met and married a few years ago and in 2012 opened a self-serve frozen yogurt shop start-up in Santa Fe. They employ eight part-time helpers during the busy summer months, and about five employees during the rest of the year.

Having a flexible workforce is important in their line of work, given the tourism flux in the region. Things are going well for the couple. Dave says they reached "a huge financial milestone at the end of our fourth year in business," and they're now cautiously looking into adding another location.

YOUR OPTIONS AS BOSS OF A FEW

There are generally three paths you can take with the Boss of a Few model. You can buy a franchise, purchase an existing business, or start your own business.

Buy a Franchise

If you're considering buying a franchise, it can be a good idea to look for one that requires perhaps one or two employees to start but is easily expandable as it grows. Examples include franchises in senior care, lawn maintenance, and home or commercial cleaning. In most cases, a Boss of a Few franchise will be a service-oriented business. For example, as the owner of a Maid Right franchise in Texas, Michael Schaul manages three full-time and two part-time employees out of a leased office.

Michael is a serial entrepreneur, and his story is an example of how the journey to successful entrepreneurship is not always linear. Over three decades, he moved from being a corporate oil man to a consultant (Company of One), to buying a manufacturer (Business of Many), to owning a franchise (Boss of a Few) that expanded into more than a few others (Business of Many), and he now owns a different franchise, and is again boss of a few.

When he first entered franchising, Michael started with the Boss of a Few model and eventually grew to own eight USA Baby outlets in Texas. When a host of other baby-product providers, including Amazon, saturated his previously thriving market, Michael ended up liquidating that business. He immediately started looking at Boss of a Few franchising opportunities again.

Buy an Existing Business

If you're looking at buying an existing business on the Boss of a Few model, keep in mind that it could be ideal to inherit some employees from the previous owner, making your transition to ownership that much smoother (if they are great employees, that is).

New entrepreneur Michael Croteau certainly could have used some competent legacy employees when he bought the Cottages at Tower Hill in rural New Hampshire. He sold his house in California at the same time as inking the purchase of the hospitality business on the other side of the country. Michael and his fiancée, Tina, ended up having to leave their moving van unpacked as they rushed to check a long line of customers into their twelve cabins, RV park, and camp-site. It was high vacation season, a less than ideal moment to start their new business, which didn't come with any staff.

Start Your Own Business

If you have a good idea for a new (or improved) product or a service that's currently underserved in your market, choosing the route of building a Boss of a Few business from the ground up can be a good model. Being a solopreneur may inhibit how quickly you can gain traction in the marketplace, especially if you are first to market with your product or service. However, if you do choose to start a business, be sure to start small, hiring the minimum number of employees you require and adding staff only as needed.

PROS OF THE BOSS OF A FEW MODEL
Increased Everything

The differences between the Company of One and Boss of a Few models can be measured in multiples. When you add a quality employee, you potentially double your output or production. Add another quality employee, and the production triples. Of course, there are a number of variables with regard to employee roles, but in general, the more "right fit" hands on deck, the more money can come through the door!

Hands On

Regardless of your experiences in the corporate world, you'll find running a small business totally different—more intimate, more immediate, and often more rewarding. When employees succeed under your guidance, your work satisfaction can be very high.

Freedom and Flexibility

A funny thing happens when you have employees and you're the top dog: you can actually afford to step away for a while! Whether it's for a couple of days or a couple of weeks, your absence will not mean the business crumbles (as is the case with the Company of One). Smart, capable, and well-trained employees are the best insurance policy you can buy.

CONS OF THE BOSS OF A FEW MODEL
Increased Everything

Yep, this has its downside too. More employees means more office-space overhead, more salaries, more benefits, more training, and the need for some type of payroll accounting or HR management. In short, more cost, more hassle, more time.

Stress

While having employees and a collaborative team atmosphere can be rewarding, it can also add stress to your life. All of a sudden, you're responsible not only for your own family's well-being, but also for your employees', and their spouses' and children's, well-being. That can be a lot of pressure, especially in the first year, when breaking even is considered a success. Be sure to have the right support in place to help you deal with emotional stress. Stress disables, even kills— and it sure doesn't make for a fun workplace.

Impact Is Capped

Having only a few employees can be limiting after a few years. Your business may hit a growth ceiling—the point when you realize how much greater an impact you *could* have on the market, on the community, on your family's well-being and your employees' well-being, if only you could grow!

BOSS OF A FEW CHECKLIST

☐ Hire more employees only as the workload warrants.

☐ Franchising can be a relatively easy way for a quick start.

☐ Plan for the time to properly train your employees and put the appropriate business operation systems in place.

☐ Pace yourself, moving carefully and methodically through the start-up steps required, following professional advice.

CHAPTER 6

Business of Many

The "Business of Many" model is a considerably different entrepreneurial animal from the Boss of a Few or Company of One. Obviously there are going to be a lot more moving parts to manage—including more employees (five or more); a larger office, retail, or other commercial space; and often expanded services or product offerings.

WHY THE BUSINESS OF MANY MODEL COULD BE A GOOD FIT FOR YOU

The Business of Many model may be the place to start if the following description fits you:

- You are motivated by challenge, complexity, and frequent change.

- The higher cost of this business model doesn't intimidate you.

- Whatever you did in your corporate career prepared you well to steer a decent-sized ship and manage its crew.

- You have tremendous drive and work ethic, and are very confident in your business vision and how to get there.

- You are comfortable surrounding yourself with employees who have strengths that you do not.

YOUR OPTIONS FOR A BUSINESS OF MANY
Buy a Scalable Franchise

To start off, you can buy a franchise that requires between six and ten employees to launch. This baseline employee range is fairly typical for quick-service and fast-casual food concepts, as well as for retail businesses such as fitness or clothing franchises.

Buy an Existing Business

If you purchase an existing business that requires a considerable staff to run, ideally you will

- inherit at least a few good employees from the previous owner,

- reduce your learning curve by taking advantage of existing operations and business momentum,

- and have the potential to become profitable more quickly.

Examples of buying an existing Business of Many include taking over a neighborhood bar, independent coffee shop, specialty retail store, or a more industrial service-oriented business.

Daniel Knak drew on more than fifteen years' experience in operational and sales roles at electronic manufacturers when he decided to take over ownership of R&B Contract Manufacturing, a thirty-nine-hundred-square-foot plant and sixteen-hundred-square-foot warehouse in Eyota, Minnesota. In the case of this company, which specializes in custom circuit-board assemblies and control-panel manufacturing, legacy employees were a vital component, since highly skilled technicians were required to build and install its products.

If Daniel had been forced to look for these highly skilled workers, he would have experienced damaging downtime. After all, existing customers expect business as usual—a factor that complicates the transition of ownership of a larger company. It is not insurmountable, just an example of the variables that might arise when buying an existing Business of Many.

Start Your Own Business

For obvious reasons, this option doesn't present itself too often—a business start-up grows from a seed and therefore usually starts with only one, or a few, employees.

However, if you are starting up a labor-intensive business, such as a production facility, your new venture might follow this model. For example, Andrew Caplinger's seafood market start-up employed ten workers right out of the gate—many hands are needed to buy fish, unpack it, prepare it, sell it (retail side), serve it (restaurant side), drive it around (catering truck), and perform the plethora of other functions such a business entails.

PROS OF THE BUSINESS OF MANY
More Money

The bigger your company, the more return on investment you can get—assuming your business is well run, of course, and that you have a product or service that people want to buy. Sheer economics will indicate that while the front end costs (payroll, rental or purchase of space, inventory, etc.) are higher, this level of infrastructure can result in greater profits and more money to reinvest in the business for future growth.

New Hiring Gets Easier

Once you grow past a handful of employees, things actually start to get easier—changes in payroll aren't as drastic, and operational efficiencies start to surface. You may be hiring multiple people to do the same job, such as sales or customer service; in those cases, employees can start to train and mirror each other without you having to start from the ground up with each new hire.

Even More Flexibility

The freedom and flexibility experienced with the Boss of a Few model increases with the Business of Many. If you've laid the groundwork for operational efficiencies, having more employees means you can choose to do less or, at the very least, set hours that work around you and your family's schedule. Having a Business of Many also enables you to focus more on high-level strategy, such as growth management and developing new lines of business and new markets. As the brain behind the business, you need the time to devote to this.

Creating Jobs

In these challenging economic times—when full-time stable employment opportunities are shrinking—the ability to give back to your community can be very rewarding. Think of all the families your business positively impacts, and the businesses and organizations they, in turn, support (charities, sports activities, etc.). You've started a chain reaction of local prosperity; that's quite an accomplishment!

CONS OF THE BUSINESS OF MANY
More Stress

Of course, having an impact on other people's working lives and their families' lives is also quite a responsibility. You may need to provide health insurance and other benefits to your employees, to ensure their quality of life. Then there's emotional pressure to keep the business thriving—you don't want to let all those people down. Pressure can be a great motivator, but it can also cripple you with anxiety if you don't find a healthy way of dealing with stress.

Growth Management

Growth management is an ongoing challenge for a Business of Many (less so if you've engaged with a franchise system that has specific parameters). You'll need to make tough decisions, such as when to hire more people, when to graduate to a larger office or retail space, whether to expand your territory, whether to launch that new product or service, and so on. There is some wisdom to the platitude "He who hesitates is lost." Timing is often key, and, to quote another cliché, striking while the iron is hot can be vital to well-managed growth.

BUSINESS OF MANY CHECKLIST

❑ Investigate quick-service food (and some retail businesses) as franchise opportunities.

❑ Where possible, get like employees to train each other (i.e., job shadowing).

❑ Use the time freed up by having more staff to work on strategy to keep the business growing.

❑ Invest in your ongoing business education—online, in person, at school, etc.—to stay current with best practices in marketing, sales, operations, and the like.

PART III
To Build or Buy? That Is the Question
....

The road to successful entrepreneurship has many forks, and deciding which one to take depends largely on self-awareness of your strengths and limitations, both professionally and personally, as well as arming yourself with as much information, about as many business options, as possible.

In this section, you'll get a look at the two ways you can start a business: namely, *buy* one or *build* your own. We explore the pros and cons of each choice, so you can research your options with your eyes wide open.

CHAPTER 7

....

Buying a Franchise

M any first-time entrepreneurs gravitate toward buying a franchise. The franchise "promise" is that if as a franchise owner you follow their roadmap—including their systems and processes and marketing tactics—you will likely do well. (And if you wish to do things your way, well, franchisors don't allow it.)

When you think of franchising, you may automatically picture a McDonald's or other food-service chain. While that's one type of opportunity, there are many others you may not realize are out there, including services such as fitness, accounting, coaching, cleaning houses or offices, painting, computer repair, and lots more.

When you're considering a franchise, here are some preliminary questions to keep in mind:

- What industry interests you and is desirable in your area—of expertise and geographically?

- How much money are you willing and able to invest?

- Are you more comfortable starting with the Company of One, Boss of a Few, or Business of Many model?

- Can you be comfortable working within an established system where you don't have the freedom to do many things your own way?

- How do you feel about having a model wherein you share a percentage of your profits with a head office?

- Is a franchise something you can really get behind in terms of personal interest?

Tom Walker, forty-one, can speak to that last point. He and his brother Richard, forty-seven, have been fitness buffs all their lives, so investing in a Koko FitClub territory in Colorado—along with Richard's wife, Linda—makes sense.

"You have to have a genuine interest in what you do," says Tom. "If you are looking at a franchise just to generate revenue, people will pick up on that." Richard practiced as a chiropractor for a long time, but he folded his business to join Tom in the fitness club. Linda's interests as a family physician also fit with the franchise, although she's kept her practice and is a silent investor in Koko FitClub.

When they researched fitness franchise opportunities, Richard and Tom learned of Koko's "digital gym" concept and became convinced of its unique value in the industry. Tom says they didn't even consider starting their own gym from scratch because "it wouldn't be as niche" as the high-tech Koko. He adds, "We wanted a proven, established system that had been field tested." With more than 116 locations since 2007, the Koko FitClub franchise fit the bill.

THE FRANCHISE CONSULTANT

If you're not as sure as the Walker brothers, deciding what kind of franchise might suit you can be daunting. There are literally thousands of franchise systems in the United States. You may want to consider working with a professional franchise consultant. It costs nothing; the franchise consultant gets paid by the franchisor you select.

The franchise consultant will conduct extensive interviews with you to determine what's really important to you, your spouse and family, and what you're looking to achieve. Once the assessment is completed, the consultant will present you with franchise options that feel like a good fit for you. The franchise consultant can also help you navigate the due diligence process with the franchisor you choose.

Information about a franchise consultant was included in the exit package Slade Gleaton, fifty-one, was given by his employer. When his job was eliminated, Slade says he and his wife, Lori, forty-nine, had already been talking for years about self-employment and thought, "If we don't do it now, we never will." They worked with the franchise consultant "to whittle down our choices," says Slade.

The couple looked at many franchising opportunities that "didn't resonate with us," says Slade. They gravitated toward the PRO Martial Arts franchise because it fit with their backgrounds and interests. Lori worked in education, so teaching martial arts was a good fit for her. Slade had worked at a nonprofit organization, so he knew about "hiring people who are looking for passion in their work," and martial arts is an activity that people tend to be very passionate about.

Although it is a definite advantage to believe in and enjoy the product or service you base your new business upon, it's not enough. You still need to invest the time to learn everything you can about the specific franchise—including its culture and company values, its success rate, longevity, revenues, and more.

A franchise consultant, should you choose to work with one, can help you get past the shiny exterior of all those franchisor websites, magazines, testimonial videos, podcasts, social media, and events. You'll want to spot any "deal breakers" as early as possible, so you don't waste time going down the wrong franchise path.

When you've found the franchise you wish to purchase, it's time to reach out and connect with a franchisor and begin the due diligence process. Any franchise system, by law, makes this process much easier because it's required to share with you its franchise disclosure document (FDD), which outlines all the business facts, figures, and costs inherent in the franchise. Of course, you can and should augment this due diligence by talking with other franchisees about their experiences. This is known as the "validation" process.

HOW TO GET THE MOST FROM VALIDATION

1. Contact as many franchisees as possible—ideally in person; if not, by phone. Sample a wide variety of

franchisees—those who have been with the system a year, five years, even those who have been with the franchise since its inception. You are seeking feedback on what you can expect at *all* stages of the business cycle.

2. Discover their pain points: When you go past the surface and ask incisive questions, you'll get incisive answers. Franchisees are usually forthcoming with the information you seek. Be direct and specific, and ask open-ended questions such as, What has been the biggest unexpected challenge? What advice do they wish they had been given when they started?

3. Keep your perspective: The pain points and highlights you hear about won't necessarily be the same ones you will experience with the franchise. Ask questions to determine whether your lifestyle, motivations, and risk tolerance are a good match with the franchise culture they describe. How well do you identify with the franchise personally or with its market? Consider these things before jumping to conclusions either way.

PROS OF BUYING A FRANCHISE
Established Road Map

A franchise comes with a well-paved, well-traveled road to follow, where many obstacles have been cleared by the franchisor. For a first-time business owner, having a proven road map can be invaluable.

Built-In Support

Entrepreneurship can get lonely, but franchising provides a unique infrastructure of support. Not only do you have the franchisor to lean on for guidance, you also have a network of franchisees who serve as a peer support group—to share business tips and sometimes just to socialize with people going through the same experience.

Quick Start

The result of franchising's proven road map and built-in support is a significantly shortened ramp-up period—that is, the amount of time it takes to break even on your initial investment. "Franchising, for me, is a great option for a quick start," says Michael Schaul. "The franchisor is like having a partner." When he bought into the USA Baby franchise, Michael recalls, he'd "never done retail before—USA Baby helped me learn that very quickly."

Less Perceived Risk

A tried-and-true business model not only increases your ability to succeed; it increases the probability that a bank will take a chance on you should you decide to apply for a business loan. Banks favor the proven track record of a franchisor over, say, a business start-up.

Flexibility of Owner's Time

You could experience greater flexibility in your work schedule with a franchise—given that processes, systems, suppliers, and marketing are already in place. For example, the martial arts franchise purchased by Slade and Lori Gleaton "supports semi-absenteeism," he says. That's been important to the couple. In addition to their busy lifestyle raising kids, Slade continues to work as a part-time land Realtor, and Lori teaches on the side. They've hired a program director to run the franchise, and they employ two other full-time employees and three contract employees who are martial arts experts.

Training and Operational Support

Franchisors routinely provide some level of training before and during the launch of your franchise business. For someone brand new to entrepreneurship or franchising and—like Dan Murphy of Syracuse—more than a little scared by the idea, training before and during the purchase can be the deal maker.

Dan and his spouse were flown out to "discovery days" hosted by CertaPro Painters before he bought a franchise. At the franchisor headquarters, in a classroom environment, CertaPro "really broke down their business plan, what to expect in the first three years. They went into their own software . . . full disclosure of the mechanics of their business," he recalls. In the evenings after group dinners, Dan and other prospects met CertaPro franchise owners in a "speed dating" setting where they could pepper them with business questions.

Franchises generally offer access to peers after the purchase as well. Don Rollins likes that every week he and a half-dozen other Signworld franchise owners brainstorm, share ideas and tips, and even refer business to one another. That kind of support is hard to beat, and not so easy to find should you go the route of a business start-up or buying an existing business.

CONS OF BUYING A FRANCHISE
Fees and Royalties

With franchising you get a proven system and processes, as well as a known brand, so it should come as no surprise that you have to pay for those benefits. Franchisors require franchisees to pay an initial fee up front and usually an ongoing royalty fee (and potentially marketing fees) each month. Often the royalty fee is smaller in the first year or two and increases as you get your footing as a franchisee. It should be noted that the revenue-sharing model differs from franchise to franchise, so do your homework on each franchisor you're considering.

Locked-Down Commitment

Most franchisors structure the agreement with franchisees by assigning a term of license usage: e.g., a ten- or twenty-year agreement. Once you sign such an agreement, it's difficult to make changes.

Built-In Parameters

To control quality and consistency in the customer experience, franchisees must adhere to a stringent set of guidelines and operate within the franchisor's parameters. The restrictions extend to marketing, support services, and suppliers. There's not much room to be creative or to do things "your own way."

That was a turnoff for Amy Shellart and Christina Hesse when they decided to operate a healthy-vending-machine business. The couple started looking at franchises, but they abandoned that course of action because they wanted to be able to pick and choose the drinks and foods to go into the vending machines. "With franchises, you have to use their products," says Amy, "so there isn't as much flexibility." Instead, they bought Naturals2Go vending machines from Vend Tech International, and Amy's family shops locally to stock them with products.

Geographic Restrictions

Franchisees are often required to purchase a territory—an area determined geographically. By contract, franchisees cannot seek business outside this predetermined area without buying more territory from the franchisor if it is available.

FRANCHISING CHECKLIST

❑ Give some serious thought to how much doing things "your way" matters to you, particularly when it comes to processes, marketing, supplies, and other operational procedures.

❑ Talk to other franchise owners to see what their experience has been like.

❑ Consider hiring a professional franchise consultant to narrow your choices and to help you through due diligence with the franchisor.

For more information about franchising, visit yourbestboss.com/franchising.

CHAPTER 8

....

Buying an Existing Business

Buying an existing business lies in the middle ground between the off-the-shelf predictability of franchising and the DIY individuality of a business start-up. (Resale franchise opportunities, in which you buy out people who want out of their franchise license agreements early, fall under the category of buying an existing business.) Regardless of what type of existing business you buy, here are some crucial steps.

WORK WITH BUSINESS BROKERS

A business broker is an excellent resource to help you identify businesses for sale in your area. Unfortunately, businesses tend to be marketed exclusively by one broker at a time, which means you will need to work with several business brokers.

Be sure you check the reputation of the business brokers—their references, their standing with the Better Business Bureau, their reputation in your community. The better the broker's reputation, the more likely it is that he or she is representing quality businesses.

Once you've selected your business brokers, and they've found some businesses that appeal to you, be sure to do the following:

DIG INTO THE VALUATION OF THE BUSINESS

Businesses are usually valued at a multiple of the revenue generated, aka "owner benefit." About 2.5–3.5 times the owner benefit is a reasonable asking price. If it's going for much more or less than that, you should dig deeper to understand why.

HAVE YOUR ACCOUNTANT CHECK UNDER THE HOOD

You should get a copy of the last three years of the business's tax returns and accounting records. Have your own accountant check to see if there is anything being done to overly inflate the owner benefit.

GET OTHER BROKERS' ADVICE

Even if you think you've identified the business you'd like to buy, it doesn't hurt to get the opinion of other local business brokers. Take your time, do the research, and consult with your advisors. Better to invest time and money now than to deal with surprises down the line!

FIND OUT WHY THE OWNER IS SELLING

When investigating a business, it pays to pay attention to *why* the owner is selling. Sometimes people may be forthcoming with this information—maybe she is retiring to Florida or he hurt his back and can no longer do the required work. Other times you may get an evasive "I'm ready to move on." The latter suggests there may be an underlying problem. Be a little suspicious, and keep researching. What is the state of the industry the business belongs to? Is the business based on a novelty or trend that could be on its way out, and the owner wants to jump ship just in time? Do your research, but also listen to your gut if the pieces still don't seem to add up after you've taken the due diligence as far as you (legally) can.

The same questions apply if you're exploring a franchise resale. Figure out why the franchisee is unloading one or more units. Does he want out because the product or service is underperforming in the market? Observe his business, ask around, find out!

No matter how much rapport, or perceived trust, you may have with the seller, check the status of your prospective business with the Better Business Bureau. Are there complaints? Was the company ever involved in a lawsuit? You can be sure that an existing business will come to you with its reputation intact—whether that reputation is good or bad. Google the company name; read all the online reviews you find; talk to people in the community who've had any dealings with the business to see their impressions of the business, its owner, employees, and premises.

Those conversations should include competitors of the existing business you're considering. (No need to disclose that you're thinking of buying a competitive business.) Ask about their pains and challenges, the spending habits of local consumers, the best part of their business, etc. If they won't speak with you, observe their business firsthand, quietly from the wings.

POTENTIAL RED FLAGS IN BUYING A BUSINESS
Seller's Valuation versus Bank's Valuation

Business valuation is a necessary part of any buying/selling process, and there are always two perspectives to business valuation:

1. *Bank's or accountant's valuation.* Impartial and complete; their calculations are based on what's happened with the business in the past and present, not the future.

2. *Valuation by the business owner.* The seller is obviously going to want to put as high a value on his business as possible. He also might be selling his life's passion, so his emotion plays a part in the valuation. The owner also tends to focus on *projected* revenues, which are never a sure thing.

The Owner Is Key to Sustainability

You need to find out just how much the success of the business is tied to the present owner. When that owner leaves, will the value and credibility of the business exit too? (Incidentally, a business named after its previous owner is not something you necessarily want to change; the name may be an asset if it brings brand recognition and a following.)

Employees Leave with the Former Owner

Since you do not want the former owner to take the best and brightest employees with him when he leaves, it's a good idea to sign a "noncompete agreement" to protect yourself. That way he doesn't set up a competing business across town with those employees. You obviously can't force legacy employees to stay, but you should entice the *good* ones—the employees customers are familiar with and enjoy—to do so, to ensure continuity of business.

Seller Stays on Too Long

Some transactions involve a "seller carry" condition in which you buy the business in installments according to a payment schedule. This can be helpful if the business starts to struggle because you essentially have a partner to help you make it work if you can't get a loan. This kind of arrangement (also known as an "owner carry") generally runs from one to five years.

Be wary of the specific circumstances: if you give the seller any kind of extended say in how you run your business be sure it's firmly in *your* favor. You may want to consider a shorter-term consulting arrangement—anywhere from thirty days to six months—wherein the seller sticks around to ensure that you're up to speed and the transition of ownership is smooth. Get professional advice on this.

PROS TO BUYING AN EXISTING BUSINESS
Less Perceived Risk

There is less risk involved with buying an existing business than in starting up a new one because, having done your due diligence, you've chosen a business that has already proven successful on some level. You are buying an established location, amenities, staff, and, most important, an established customer base and reputation in the community.

Quicker ROI

Getting a return on your investment (ROI) as quickly as possible is a definite advantage of buying an existing business, especially one with a long history and a strong financial ledger. Even if you've incurred debt in purchasing the business, its existing cash flow will enable you to break even and pay off any business debt that much faster.

A fast, substantial ROI was important to Steven Tang, fifty-one, when he decided to leave his fifteen-year career as an IT manager for a major financial-services firm and become an entrepreneur. He wanted to go as big as he could afford—so after looking at many opportunities, he and his girlfriend, Meiyan Lin, thirty-seven, decided to buy an established business—a multimillion-dollar deal. They bought the Duncan Corners Bottle Shop, a liquor store in Braselton, Georgia, including its eleven-thousand-square-foot building.

"We were tired of working for other people," says Steven, adding that he was getting to the age where he might not get the chance again. The couple moved to Georgia from Virginia after the multi-million-dollar deal closed. "It took months to negotiate," says Steven, who did exhaustive due diligence, including poring over the previous owner's books to establish the cash flow.

Steven says he and Meiyan, who has a background in the restaurant industry, enjoy having flexible hours as business owners (they have six full-time employees, carryovers from the former owner), as well as the opportunity for growth in the perennially stable industry of selling liquor. "It's uncharted waters for me; I'm still learning," he says. "But the business is stable." He's confident that buying an existing business was the right entrepreneurial move for him.

More Access to Capital

Steven and Meiyan discovered that getting approved for a bank loan was relatively easy when buying an existing business. The liquor store had a proven track record of turning a profit for years—a fact that the bank clearly liked. Steven's bank loan was approved in late 2014, so the improving U.S. economic climate was also a positive factor. Aside from the loan, they needed to find another source of funding. Steven learned how he could leverage his 401(k) for the business purchase. He worked with my company, CatchFire Funding, to roll over his retirement funds, procure a bank loan, and set up his and Meiyan's new company, Tanglin Corporation.

CONS TO BUYING AN EXISTING BUSINESS
Business Baggage

There are bound to be unknowns or curveballs with any venture, but existing businesses tend to be more of a wildcard, especially compared to franchises, since franchisors are bound by law to disclose all business details in their franchise disclosure document. (And of course if you start your own business, no one has come before you so there is nothing to disclose.) An existing business often has years of history—let's call it the equivalent of the emotional baggage someone brings to a personal relationship. That history (ledger, reputation) could affect you somewhere down the line.

It Takes Time

Searching for the perfect existing business to buy can sometimes feel like waiting for the stars to align—unlike a start-up, which you can choose to open anytime you like, or a franchise, where the franchisor is always eager to get you up and running. You can save some time by working with professionals—business brokers, a business attorney, small business funding experts. But be patient; you may have to kiss a lot of frogs before you find your perfect match.

Download a guide to finding the right existing business at yourbestboss.com/greatbusiness.

BUYING AN EXISTING BUSINESS CHECKLIST

❑ Work with several business brokers to find a suitable company and help you negotiate the deal.

❑ Don't overlook franchise resale opportunities.

❑ Trust the bank's valuation of the business, not the seller's valuation.

❑ Talk to employees of the company, people in the community, competitors.

Buying an Existing Business

☐ Be careful about what stays and what goes with the seller.

☐ Get the seller to sign a noncompete agreement through your attorney.

☐ Get professional advice on an "owner carry" arrangement.

CHAPTER 9

....

Building Your Own Business

Building a business from the ground up is both exhilarating and somewhat terrifying—a venture with none of the security, rules, or comforting track record that comes with buying a franchise or an existing company. Fortunately, there are specific actions you can take to minimize the risk and fear factor when building your own business.

IMPROVE UPON A PRODUCT OR SERVICE THAT'S IN DEMAND

It's unlikely that you'll find a product or service *no one* has ever offered before—few of us are inventors! However, your community could be underserviced: certain products or services may be hard to find, or perhaps the quality of those products or services can be improved upon. While being first to market isn't essential for a business start-up, having a strong business plan and competitive advantage is.

When Chris Taylor started his own company, after twenty-five years working in corporate America, he wanted to capitalize on a Securities and Exchange Commission (SEC) mandate that created an IT business opportunity. Even though Chris says he was "late to market" (competitors acted on the opportunity before he did), he *improved* upon the service—modernizing and making electronic security filings more efficient. As a result, his company, P3XBRL Inc., reached $2 million in annual sales within the first three years.

INSTATE PROCESSES AND SYSTEMS

A start-up means you are not inheriting processes or systems from a preexisting business. You need to start from scratch. Even so, it's critical to get your processes and systems in place as early as you can afford to. Not only do you need processes, systems, and tools to keep track of inventory, schedules, customers, prospects, and more, you need them to be as efficient as possible. Wasting time with manual processes riddled with human error is going to put a major crimp in your profitability during your first months.

Automating your processes via software and/or online tools could cost a bit up front but will save you a great deal of time and money in the long term, and possibly even reduce the size of the staff you need to hire. The nature of your staffing arrangement may also be altered by the technology you choose. For example, P3XBRL has a "virtual" office: every one of Chris's twenty-five employees, including himself, works out of his or her home. This style may not be for everyone, or even feasible in many fields of work, but it works for the online/administrative nature of that company. To make it work, Chris invested in technology such as Microsoft Office 365 for instant messaging and other forms of communication between his remote employees and their clients.

MARKETING BEFORE SALES

Before you do *anything*, write a marketing strategy. Plan out how you're going to position and sell your product or service. Be specific about which channels you'll use to market it: online and/or print advertising, direct mail, social media, speaking engagements, referral programs, etc. Chris Taylor took an approach to sales and marketing that paid off for P3XBRL. Since his start-up was a couple of years behind the market, Chris decided not to sell to the end users (SEC registrants) but rather to the filing agents whose clients are the end users. The model proved golden. Although it has only twelve customers, P3XBRL is used by almost four hundred SEC registrants who each need the service four times a year.

Administrative support is critical to running a business, and with today's software and online tools, it's easier than ever to set up, even without in-house expertise in accounting, HR, and law. Chris notes that his company's customer relationship management (CRM) system, accounting system, and production queue are all cloud-based applications integrated into an efficient services resource planning (SRP) application that supports all the management and information requirements at P3XBRL.

HIRE PROFESSIONAL ADVISORS

Hiring great service providers is vital when you set up a business. They might include a financial advisor, like myself, who specializes in rolling over 401(k) funds to finance business start-ups, a business attorney, an accountant, or any other professional who can help you do things *correctly the first time*. Skimp on these costs at the early stage, and it will end up costing you in preventable mistakes.

FORM STRATEGIC REFERRAL PARTNERSHIPS

Part of the beauty of being a business owner is figuring out how you can leverage the talents of other people, such as complementary businesses, organizations, and individuals who are not in direct competition with you. Referral partnerships can be integral for a new business. For example, if you install marble countertops, align yourself with other local tradespeople such as tile setters and cabinet installers. Your customers will likely have a need for more than one of those services, and the more referrals you can give—and get back—the better. Remember, though, referrals take time and relationship skills. It's not a matter of a "quick ask" but rather a building of mutual trust and respect.

Julie Richter is an old hand at building relationships. The owner of Compass Insurance Group is on the board of directors of the Missoula Businesswomen's Network (and also chair of its empowerment committee), the Missoula County Relay for Life, Missoula's Hospice Care Foundation, and, until recently, the Missoula County DUI Task Force.

"I believe in the Golden Rule, and the importance of building relationships in all aspects of life, personal and professional," Julie says. "I can usually tell who is involved in community events for their business, and who does it just because it's the right thing to do."

FIND A NICHE

It isn't enough to be very good at what you do; if your market is glutted with your product or service, you probably aren't going to be as profitable as you'd like. "Make sure it isn't a dime-a-dozen type of business," advises Andrew Caplinger, whose seafood market is the only business of its kind in Indianapolis. He adds, "I see a lot of entrepreneurs doing what a lot of other people are doing. . . . Find a niche in your market, something you know extremely well and are really good at." Also determine where there is sufficient demand.

PROS OF BUILDING YOUR OWN BUSINESS
Personal Freedom

Few things are more rewarding or liberating than seeing your ideas manifest and come to life. There is never a truer sense of a business being your "baby" than when you build it from the ground up with your own blood, sweat, and tears. If you were looking to get away from the constraints of the corporate world, you can't get much further than this.

A serial entrepreneur herself, Julie Richter notes, "When people are their own boss, they will put more effort into what they do, more excitement, more passion. . . . I don't like people telling me what to do, and I find most people don't either." She adds, "I believe that most people do better as entrepreneurs [than as employees]. They create their own legacy."

Make It Up as You Go

Unlike with a franchise or even an existing business, building from the ground up means there are no limitations or preconceived notions about how the business should be run. That independence was very important to Dave Christianson. When his wife, Pattie, came home one day inspired by a self-serve frozen yogurt shop she'd visited, they started looking at various options, including several "fro-yo" franchises. But they decided they wanted more independence in creating the atmosphere and product than the franchise model allowed. "We feel that frozen yogurt is just a commodity, whereas our product is happiness," says Dave.

The Christiansons also visited more than a hundred fro-yo stores across the United States, "And we've only found one other mom-and-pop shop like ours," says Dave, proudly. Their downtown Santa Fe business, called Frogurt, is decked out with big-screen TVs for gaming and watching cartoons, as well as surround-sound music indoors and outdoors.

Limitless Growth

When you build your own business, the only limitations are the ones you place on yourself. You alone determine how big you want to get or how small you want to stay. You also decide how specialized you want to be or how much you diversify the business. The Christiansons are looking into a second Frogurt location, and they don't need to go through any franchisor, or scour the books of an existing business, to do it.

CONS OF BUILDING YOUR OWN BUSINESS
Ramp-Up Time

In contrast to buying a franchise or an existing business, building from the ground up requires you to lay all the groundwork described above, and that takes time—sometimes lots of it: Time to find the right business advisors. Time to build in those processes and systems. Time to do sufficient market research on demand for your idea. Think about it—without a recipe to follow, it takes longer to create anything, whether dinner or a business. You need patience to get through the critical, painstaking prelaunch and ramp-up phases (generally the first two years).

You're on an Island

A brand-new business doesn't have history—such as legacy employees that might come with the purchase of a preexisting business—and it definitely does not have the luxury that franchisees have in the network of fellow owners to reach out to and lean on for much-needed support. As the owner of a new business, you're largely alone. Maybe you have a spouse or other family member working with you, or maybe your start-up is larger than that and you have a few supportive employees, but still you won't find much overlap between your former corporate circles and your new role as an entrepreneur. Brace yourself for some serious stretches of solitude.

BUILDING YOUR OWN BUSINESS CHECKLIST

❑ Find a niche market that is underserviced in your region.

❑ Put significant time into building the right processes and systems, no matter how boring you find it.

❑ Technology can enable both "virtual" and actual offices.

❑ Hire the best service providers (attorney, financial advisor, etc.) you can afford.

❑ Build reciprocal referral partnerships in your community.

For more information about building your own business, go to yourbestboss.com/startup.

CHAPTER 10

To Partner or Not?

You may be wondering, Should I go it alone when I start my own venture, or should I get a business partner? How do I know who is reliable to partner with, and how do I properly go about forming a partnership?

You're right to wonder. You'll find no shortage of cautionary tales about business partnerships gone terribly wrong. But of course there are many examples of thriving partnerships too. And there are different types of business partnerships—with an outsider, with family, with a friend.

OUTSIDE PARTNERSHIP

An outside partnership means a partnership with someone who isn't within your trusted circle of family and friends. In such a partnership you are ideally seeking a perfect balance of

- "money man," who brings capital to the partnership, and

- "operations guy," who understands, and maybe does, the day-to-day running of the business.

Regardless of what type of equity your potential outside partner provides (money or sweat), be sure you examine *all* aspects of the person, not just his or her cash and/or skill set. Check his or her character too. Get references. Ask around. After all, this is someone with whom your fortunes may be linked for some time to come. And ask yourself how you feel. You may have to work alongside this person every day.

Setting expectations—up front and in a legally binding agreement—is critical, especially if an arrangement of sweat equity versus capital is brought to the partnership. No matter what someone says at the start of a business partnership, you do not want the "money man" to feel like he is more entitled to ownership than the partner who brings less capital.

Michael Schaul left behind a solid career with an oil company to become an entrepreneur in 1995, buying a bankrupt apparel manufacturer in Wisconsin. "I needed money," says Michael. "Banks weren't going to loan me the millions I needed to buy and operate this business." So his investment banker found Michael a partner who had both money and some exposure to the apparel industry.

What this "money man" also had, Michael found out later, were "other businesses that were his priority."

He advises other entrepreneurs: "If you're getting into bed with someone, you need background checks. . . . I may have looked elsewhere [for a partner] if my investment banker had done that. He would have found a couple of red flags." Overall, Michael's business partnership "went as successfully as it could." They managed to sell the business for a nice profit within five years, but Michael learned some valuable lessons for the next business partnership he embarked upon.

PARTNERSHIP WITH A FRIEND

Although conventional wisdom holds that one shouldn't mix money and friendship, this is, in fact, the exact nature of the partnership that has worked out the best for Michael Schaul. When he took on his best friend, Jeff Briggs, as his next business partner, Michael knew the character of his partner very well—his personality, work ethic, and how much time he put into other endeavors.

Michael, Jeff, and their wives met in Wisconsin, where their kids went to school together. When the Schauls moved to Dallas to buy a USA Baby franchise, Michael brought on Jeff as a partner—first for one store, and then for the whole business, which was worth $8 million within four years. They ended up selling off the business in 2014, in what Michael calls "a very successful liquidation sale," after the market became saturated with baby products. Jeff jumped out of the business in 2012, soon after the first two of their nine stores were liquidated.

"My wife said we should never have brought Jeff and his family down to Dallas since the business didn't work out," says Michael. "But if you ask them, they are so happy they did it. They moved from small-town Wisconsin to a thriving city, the kids got great schools," and Jeff and Michael remain best friends. Today Jeff is thriving as a

Smoothie King franchise owner in the Dallas area, Michael as a master franchisee for Maid Right in Frisco, Texas.

Friend or stranger, Michael stresses that "a business partnership is like a marriage: it's a long-term commitment." You should treat the start of a partnership as seriously and carefully as you would a marriage proposal.

FAMILY PARTNERSHIP

As the stories in this book indicate, it is common to see couples partnering in business. Less commonly, an individual might partner with his or her parent or adult siblings. To a large extent, especially in middle age, family members are reevaluating where they're at in life and in their most intimate relationships. Business dreams can be particularly satisfying when shared with loved ones.

However, a family business partnership brings with it certain unique challenges. For a married or common-law couple, working and living together 24-7 can be a stressful situation and, if not handled well, can lead to problems in the relationship as well as in the business. There are other factors to consider before starting a business with a family member.

All Your Income in One Basket
Spouses are sometimes leery of putting both incomes in one basket— i.e., the new business. With no fallback income in place, lean times in the business will mean lean times at home. Having dependents, such as kids or elderly parents, makes this scenario even more worrisome.

Some new entrepreneur-spouses decide that one person should

keep his or her day job, for a while at least. Amy Shellart has kept her corporate career while her life and business partner, Christina Hesse, who is also a stay-at-home mom, gets their company started. Christina is busy placing their ten natural-food vending machines in Springfield, Missouri, businesses. Once momentum has built, their expectation is that Amy will join the business full time.

While Amy and Christina's start-up costs were minimal—just purchasing the vending machines and products—the Olenicks needed Mark's income to bankroll the fairly expensive start-up of Luke's Cukes (about $100,000 in renovations to a century-old general store, $75,000 in pickling equipment, and other costs). As a result, Mark's leap to entrepreneurship was more like a straddle: for the first five years, he worked nights and weekends at the existing family business, while his wife, Tracey, ran the food start-up.

The Kids of Entrepreneurs

Children can add a layer of stress to a marriage and business partnership. However, they don't have to if both partners are committed to involving the kids as much as possible in the business (where appropriate, of course).

Slade Gleaton works the day shift and his wife, Lori, works in the evenings at the PRO Martial Arts franchise they bought in Charleston, South Carolina. Their three teenagers aren't always so pleased with Mom and Dad's new entrepreneurship. "There's been some pressure around the time the business is taking," says Slade. "We talk to the kids a lot about how we need to get beyond the start-up point." Until then, their two youngest teens at least feel connected and involved by helping out at the franchise.

Amy and Christina got their preteen kids involved in naming their business, taste testing, and shopping for food and drinks to stock the vending machines.

For a year, while working on the rapidly expanding pickle business, Tracey Olenick packed up four kids, two still in diapers, and regularly drove six hours across state, from their home in Lititz, Pennsylvania, to the new business in Venango. Making it a fun part of their lives paid off: the older Olenick kids now help out at the pickle factory, store, and café.

If your kids are teens or adults, they may be willing and able to help out in your new business. Just be sure to clearly delineate roles and responsibilities, and to comply with laws about paid employment and/or stock options for adult children.

Complementary Strengths

Objectively assessing the strengths and weaknesses that each business partner brings to the table is just as important in family partnerships as in any other. If you feel too close to your spouse to do this well, bring in a nonbiased, trusted person to help you identify and assign the soft and hard skills you and your life partner have to offer.

Tracey Olenick used her financial and accounting background to get Luke's Cukes off the ground and draws on it now to keep it profitable, while her husband Mark has leaned on the project management and communications skills he cultivated during two decades in the corporate world. In the Gleason marriage, it's the other way around: Slade handles the numbers, and Lori manages clients and staff at their martial arts franchise.

Offspring or Parent Partnership

Family business partnerships might also be formed with siblings or between parents and children. In 2005, Nick Caplinger lost the successful seafood retail business he'd founded with a nonfamily partner (the partner was stealing funds and bankrupted the business). A fish man since the age of eighteen, and a proud owner, Nick took it pretty hard, emotionally as well as financially, says his son, Andrew.

Andrew did not let this history dissuade him from starting a new family fish market, albeit some years later. Although Andrew is the primary owner, Nick, now fifty-seven, is a working partner in his son's business, which is located about ten minutes from Nick's defunct fish market, to capitalize on former customers.

"It's an interesting dynamic. I worked for Dad all my life. We work together now," says Andrew. "But all the final decisions come down to me." He's grateful that he doesn't need to look outside his trusted inner circle for business or trade expertise.

PROS OF PARTNERSHIP
Capital Infusion

Obviously, sharing the financial burden of starting a business is a big attraction. More work can get done with more partners (and more cash flow), especially at the early stages when you might not be able to afford to hire employees.

Companionship

In a partnership, you can bounce business ideas off each other and avoid the loneliness that can come with solopreneurship.

Less Risky

Each partner invests capital and/or sweat equity, minimizing the level of risk.

Divide and Conquer

With two energies—and, ideally, complementary skills—you can get more done in less time, thereby accelerating your ROI.

CONS OF PARTNERSHIP
Profit Sharing

The flip side, of course, is that you have to share the profits (as specified in the formal co-ownership agreement).

Decision Making

With a business partner, you also have to share the decision making, which obviously requires more compromise and serious negotiation and interpersonal skills. (Keep in mind that any partnership that's not fifty-fifty is not equal; somebody has leverage.)

Blurred Lines

Misunderstandings over the partners' roles in the business can happen if those roles are not clearly outlined in writing at the start. It's also important to check in with each other regularly to reassess and update those roles.

PARTNERSHIP CHECKLIST

❑ Be sure to partner with someone who has skill sets and/or assets that are complementary to your own.

❑ You and your partner don't have to be friends, but you do need to be *friendly*, day in and day out.

❑ Consider partnership as a long-term commitment that requires as much work as a good marriage, before and during.

❑ Have a business attorney draw up a formal, legally binding contract of partnership that *very clearly* states expectations and contributions, and review those expectations and contributions regularly.

❑ Perform due diligence even on your friends if considering them as business partners.

❑ Hire a professional advisor, such as a business broker, who has experience finding partners and arranging partnerships.

❑ If a couple partners, consider one spouse keeping an outside job while the business gets going, so the family has a fallback income.

PART IV

Start Your Engines!

....

So far, so good. You've narrowed down the type of business best suited to you—Company of One, Boss of a Few, or Business of Many—and you've taken a look under the hood at what each type entails.

You've also become acquainted with the different avenues you might take: single- or multiunit franchising, buying an existing business, or building your own business. And you've looked at your options for business partnerships.

That's a lot of information you've absorbed already, and it's all important knowledge that will take you go directly to "GO"—the first square in your new entrepreneurial venture.

Now let's delve into what the *operational phases* will look like in your new business as you move from prelaunch through to company maturity and, finally, to your exit strategy. It's always a good idea to have an eye on the long-term game plan, rather than keeping your head down and limiting your vision to the current phase.

CHAPTER 11

....

The Road Map: Business Planning

"If you fail to prepare, prepare to fail." That's a hackneyed business cliché because it's true. The business plan you put in place before launching your venture should be strong enough, and detailed enough, to be followed as a blueprint for at least the first couple of years of business.

Simply put, a business plan is a road map outlining the route your business intends to take in order to succeed. A business plan is needed in order to secure funding from a bank or an investor. Your business plan must be a well-structured document that clearly communicates an objective and a thorough approach to your venture.

Chris Taylor, founder of P3XBRL, which grew from a two-person to twenty-five-employee operation in its first three years, started writing a five-year business plan, including financial projections, in early 2011. Chris says there have been a few updates to the financial forecasts since then, as well as to the sales and marketing plan, but the original, overarching business plan is solid and still used to guide operations today.

A GOOD BUSINESS PLAN CONTAINS THE FOLLOWING INFORMATION:

1. Your unique selling proposition (USP): a couple of sentences encapsulating why your business will be *different* and successful.

2. Market research: why consumers in your geographic region (or nationally, if online) need more of (or a better version of) your product or service. Include unique features of your intended sales area: for example, colleges, hospitals, ethnic demographics, target groups (such as dog owners), and any other relevant information.

3. Competitive research: what companies sell similar products or services in your region; how long have they been in business, how are they doing, etc.

4. Ideal location: what size (square footage) and located near what resources (e.g., college campus, high-value residential area, etc.).

5. Staff projections: to start and in a couple of years.

6. Potential partner(s) and/or investor(s), if any.

7. Property, building, and equipment needs, including retrofitting, new build, renovation.

8. Inventory required to start: type, volume.

9. Training required (initial and ongoing) for yourself and any staff.

10. Financial projections: first year, beyond.

See page 191 for a worksheet that will help you organize your business plan's details.

FRANCHISE BUSINESS PLAN: A HEAD START

If you're considering a franchise, you'll have a head start in developing some of the budgeting and financial-forecasting data for your business plan. As mentioned, the Federal Trade Commission requires franchisors to provide all prospective franchise buyers with a franchise disclosure document (FDD), which is similar to the prospectus you might review before investing in a publicly traded corporate stock or mutual fund.

The FDD will provide you with valuable information on the following topics, and more, to help you prepare your start-up budget:

- Franchise fees

- Training fees

- Real estate fees

- Lease deposits

- Tenant improvement costs

- Furniture, fixture, and equipment costs

- Initial marketing costs

- Initial inventory costs

- Required working capital to pay for rents, utilities, and employee salaries during the early start-up period.

Detailed reading of the FDD can provide valuable information to help you prepare your cash flow projections and estimate when your business will become profitable.

You may also be able to review business plans written by your fellow franchisees. These can shed light on things like inventory, staffing, and typically slow months—all information that will help you create your own plan.

Keep in mind that there is quite a bit of research you can, and should, undertake beyond perusing the FDD and talking to other franchisees. When Tom Walker purchased his Koko FitClub franchise, he knew he needed an in-depth understanding of the market—its demographics, trends in the region—to make it profitable. That knowledge even affected his future franchising plans: after examining the data, including average incomes, he and his business partner decided to purchase a franchise territory that covers much of Douglas County, Colorado, "one of the richest counties in the US," says Tom. They plan to open their second and third franchise locations by mid-2017.

OBSERVATION IS A GREAT TEACHER

If you're starting your own business, you obviously need to craft your own business plan. And market analysis is part of doing it right. You can pay an advisory firm to perform a competitive analysis for you, but that may not be necessary. Here is a rudimentary example of how to do your own research into the local competitive landscape.

Say you're interested in opening an independent smoothie shop. It would be helpful to know how many smoothies you can expect to sell per day. To do this, find a smoothie shop in the area and simply watch how many smoothie cups leave the store in a given hour, or a given day, and get a rough idea from there. By observing comparable businesses, you can spot inefficiencies and devise ways you would do things differently. Research doesn't always mean scouring the Internet or poring over books at the library. Observation is a wonderful teacher!

After your business plan is written, there is still much to do before opening day. Don't get overwhelmed; just tackle one task at a time, get the best advice and help you can, and stay focused. You *will* get to the starting line. The checklist below should help.

CHECKLIST: BEFORE OPENING DAY

If you're buying a franchise, you will receive a full checklist of tasks to complete—with instructions on how and when to do them—once you sign your franchise license. You'll also have a network of experienced fellow franchisees to turn to during the nail-biting prelaunch phase.

Tom Walker says the 160-page handbook he got from the Koko FitClub franchise is now pretty dog-eared. He has good advice for other entrepreneurs who are counting down to opening day: "Stay focused and have plans and guidelines to follow, so you know when to implement the next step."

Needless to say, if you are starting your own business or buying an existing (nonfranchise) business, you will need to develop your own checklist. The sample below offers a general idea of the kinds of items your checklist should include.

1. Hire professional advisor team

   ❑ Accountant

   ❑ Payroll

   ❑ Legal

   ❑ Real estate

   ❑ Business mentor(s)

2. Conduct a demographic review, leading to site selection (i.e., close to campus, mall?)

3. Negotiate lease (whether office, retail, or food service)

4. Apply for building and/or construction permits

5. Make tenant improvements

6. Install furniture and/or equipment (buildout)

7. Apply for required paperwork, such as

   ❑ Business license (federal/state/county/city)

   ❑ Sales tax

   ❑ Workers' compensation

   ❑ Unemployment insurance

   ❑ Specialty registrations (e.g., food, alcohol, hospitality)

8. Purchase and install inventory control and point-of-sale system(s) if required

9. Establish a business account at your bank

10. Establish a merchant services account to accept credit cards

11. Prepare for inventory:

    ❑ Apply for supplier accounts

    ❑ Establish payment terms

    ❑ Order initial inventory

12. Prepare HR and training procedures and manuals

13. Hire employees and train them

14. Marketing:

- ☐ Mobile-friendly website

- ☐ Send press release(s) online and to local media

- ☐ Purchase e-mail delivery tool/marketing automation for your lists

- ☐ Consider a soft opening (not publicly announced) in case of errors or delays, or the need for additional employee training

- ☐ Investigate customer relationship management (CRM) systems

Andrew Caplinger says that working with a good commercial Realtor—one who really knows your desired location—made all the difference in his prelaunch stage. "We were one week away from starting construction at a different site, but the owner backed out. I was not a happy camper," says Andrew. "But a Realtor—the same person who worked with my dad at his former fish shop—called me and said there is a business closing that has the size and requirements you need." The former burrito shop, complete with walk-in cooler, exhaust hood, and drains, was perfect for Caplinger's Fresh Catch Seafood Market.

"We had been looking at more than $70,000 on a buildout at the other space. We ended up paying only $12,000 for minor retrofits to the burrito space. . . . It couldn't have turned out better," says Andrew. "Our prayer was answered that we didn't even know to pray for!" That's the value of surrounding yourself with the best professionals during the critical prelaunch phase.

PLANNING INCLUDES BUILDING BRIDGES

Reaching out to the community is also a good idea. While you're preparing for opening day, "You need to put yourself out there," says Tom Walker. Tom has been working with four local magazines to get coverage of his new gym, both editorially and through advertising. His brother, Richard, has been reaching out to the local clientele via his chiropractic practice, spreading the word about the new gym and looking for ways the business might align with other areas in health and fitness.

BUSINESS PLANNING CHECKLIST

❑ If you fail to plan, then plan to fail.

❑ Have in-depth knowledge of your market: demographics, local trends, average incomes, competitors.

❑ Make sure you procure all the licenses and permits you require.

❑ Work with a knowledgeable Realtor, attorney, business broker, etc.

❑ If needed, employees should be one of your first and most important considerations.

❑ Don't wait for your launch to build bridges in the community; find partnerships and promotion channels ahead of time.

For more information on business planning, go to yourbestboss .com/planning.

CHAPTER 12

....

Fuel Up: Finding the Funds

The way you fund your business will have a profound effect on the eventual success of your business. That's worth repeating—so please read that sentence again.

Your funding sources should be part of your business plan. You will want to know exactly where your capital will come from. This is essential for yourself and for any lending institution, should you go that route.

As a midcareer entrepreneur you have a leg up on your younger, less experienced entrepreneurial counterparts. When it comes to business funding, you have something they don't have: *options.*

You're at a point in life where you've likely amassed a pretty impressive array of things: a house; maybe a cottage, cars, boats, or other toys; investments, savings, and retirement dollars—all things that will serve you well in funding your business.

Here is an important tip: regardless of the source of your funding, *plan to borrow 10–20 percent more than your business plan dictates you'll need*. Consider this extra padding as "contingency dollars" that will help you be prepared for the unexpected—a sort of "rainy day" fund for your business.

While it's ideal to fund your new business exclusively with your own money, it often just isn't possible. Let's explore the options, both for accessing your own money and for borrowing other people's.

YOUR OWN MONEY

A good rule of thumb is to invest about *40 percent of your personal net worth* (all your assets minus all your liabilities) into your business. That includes personal savings, retirement money, and equity such as houses and boats.

PERSONAL SAVINGS

Get ready to break open the piggy bank and dip into those hard-earned savings. Personal savings are a popular way to fund a business because many people don't have other options: they don't have the credit score or collateral to qualify for a loan, nor do they have retirement funds to access. Again, this is typically the case with younger entrepreneurs. With more mature entrepreneurs, personal assets such as stocks or bonds, a second home, and other investments can be cashed out and put on the line to fund your business.

Pros of Funding with Personal Savings
You're Not in Debt

You don't have to pay anyone back in any specific amount of time. This relieves pressure for any first-time business owner trying to make ends meet, especially in the beginning.

Cons of Funding with Personal Savings
Emergencies Happen

As we all know, life is full of the unexpected. Experienced business owners know you always need to hold something back for yourself, just in case.

Underwhelming Assets

Oftentimes when people starting cashing out their assets, they discover the assets aren't actually worth as much as they'd hoped. This is often true in housing or stock markets.

Stifling Success

By limiting yourself to funding you already have, you may not be giving your business its best chance to succeed. It might be likened to operating a business while wearing handcuffs.

YOUR RETIREMENT MONEY

There are actually three ways to tap existing retirement money to fund a new business: a loan, direct withdrawal, or a self-directed 401(k). The three options vary greatly in their limitations, taxes, and penalties.

Taking a Loan from Retirement Funds

A loan taken from your retirement funds is exactly what it sounds like: a loan that must be repaid—and within a predetermined time period. The parameters and limitations surrounding this transaction make it far from ideal, but some people feel it can be a good solution to cover very short-term needs.

Pros of Taking a Loan from Retirement Funds
ALTERNATIVE CAPITAL

If you're not eligible for a conventional loan or SBA loan, taking a loan from your retirement funds can provide you with at least some of the capital you need.

Cons of Taking a Loan from Retirement Funds
BORROWING LIMITATIONS

The government has some pretty tight guidelines when it comes to borrowing from your retirement funds. In fact, you're only allowed to borrow $50,000 or up to 50 percent of your retirement funds. Many times this is not enough money to give a new business or franchise a fighting chance to survive.

PAYBACK WINDOW

Just like with a bank loan, retirement funds need to be paid back (remember, even though it's your money, it's not yet yours to access freely). You'll have to make monthly payments until the loan is paid off. Watching loan payments go out the door each month is bound to be painful for any new business owner.

YOU MUST KEEP YOUR JOB

This is often the ultimate deal breaker in the retirement-loan scenario: not only do you have to be employed to access the loan, you have to remain employed while you pay off the loan! Starting a new business while maintaining full-time employment can be extremely difficult and stressful for you and your family.

Direct Withdrawal from Retirement Funds

Taking a direct withdrawal from retirement funds is not a loan, so the money does not have to be paid back. However, the associated fees and taxes can make this option a hard pill to swallow.

Pros of Direct Withdrawal from Retirement Funds
ALTERNATIVE CAPITAL

If you're not eligible for a business loan, direct withdrawal from your retirement funds can provide you with at least some of the capital you need.

NO BORROWING LIMITATIONS

Unlike a loan from your retirement account, a withdrawal is not limited to a certain dollar amount or percentage.

Cons of Direct Withdrawal from Retirement Funds
WITHDRAWAL FEE

In order to withdraw your funds early, there is a 10 percent withdrawal fee. The more money you withdraw, the bigger the fee!

TAXES

You'll also have to pay taxes on the money you withdraw from your retirement funds. For most people, these taxes are 30–40 percent. Ouch!

Self-Directed 401(k)

A self-directed 401(k) involves rolling over your retirement money into a new 401(k) plan that allows the subsequent investment of part of those funds into your business. Although 401(k) and IRA funds are most commonly used, SEP, SIMPLE, 403(b), 457, and others are also eligible.

When you use a self-directed 401(k) to invest in your business, you are truly investing pretax dollars. You're not borrowing funds. You're not withdrawing them. Think of it this way: when you began contributing to your 401(k), you were likely investing in your employer's stock (getting company shares in return for your cash). It's the same concept when you invest in your own small business with a self-directed 401(k). You tell your retirement plan to invest in the stock of the company you believe will be the best investment for your future: your own company. Your company gets the money from the sale of its stock. Once you've invested in your company, your company has the money to start—or expand—its business.

In 2011, Dave Coleman decided to move his family to Naples, Florida, to buy a three-year-old business that was up for sale. He first went to the bank for financing, but "Because of the market conditions at that time, banks were hesitant to loan money even to those of us with the best credit," says Coleman. "I started looking for some alternative means to finance the purchase of the business."

Dave ended up rolling over his 401(k) funds instead, and he's glad he did. "It's one less payment I have to make. . . . By not having that dagger [of debt] hanging over my head, it just makes it much easier to concentrate on working on the business to make sure it becomes self-sustaining."

Because it still isn't well known, the self-directed 401(k) is like the secret weapon of the midcareer entrepreneur. Dan Murphy hadn't heard about it before, but after speaking with fellow franchise owners who had done it, he decided to roll over his 401(k) to buy his CertaPro Painters franchise. Dan rolled over about 60 percent of the 401(k) funds he'd accrued during his three decades as a corporate employee, and he also tapped into some personal savings. Then he did a second rollover of 401(k) funds in his second year of business, when cash flow got tight.

Dan's advice—which he's heard echoed by other entrepreneurs—is that "Once the business gets into a position that you can start paying the 401(k) funds back, make sure you actually do . . . so you can convert the funds back into 401(k) status."

In her research into starting up a healthy-vending-machines business, Amy Shellart asked a supplier how he funded his purchase of the vending machines. He told her about the self-directed 401(k) option. "It was a big surprise to me, but it made sense right away," says Amy. Working with our 401(k) rollover experts at CatchFire Funding, she put about half of her 401(k) funds into a corporation to start the Goodness Locker Inc.

The self-directed 401(k) was "a big leap for me," admits Amy. But it was worth it because she didn't like the other options. "I have really good credit, but I didn't want a business loan," she says. "I'd heard what an ordeal it is to get an SBA loan."

Tapping into Your IRA

When you don't have sufficient 401(k) funds or are still working for an employer and thus cannot roll over your 401(k) to your own corporation, your individual retirement account (IRA) can be a good option for funding your new business.

Michael Schaul has tapped into his IRA funds twice as an entrepreneur—first, back in 1995, when he bought a men's apparel maker, and more recently as master franchisee for Maid Right, a cleaning service. "My IRA owns Maid Right," he says.

Brian Glazer rolled over about a third of his IRA to help his wife, Jennifer Bohling, and his stepson, Justin Batte, purchase a Jimmy John's franchise in the Fort Worth, Texas, area. Because Brian and Jennifer are still working full time at their corporate jobs, rolling over Brian's IRA into their new corporation, BJJ Ventures Inc., was the best approach. Jennifer expects to leave her job in the near future and work full time at Jimmy John's, alongside her son, at which time she intends to roll over her 401(k) into the franchise.

Rolling over Brian's IRA gave the couple the cash injection required to procure an SBA loan. They needed that loan, says Jennifer, because a single unit of Jimmy John's cost them about $350,000, and they have decided to move forward with a plan to buy several more Jimmy John's locations.

Slade Gleaton rolled over the bulk of his IRA to finance the purchase of his PRO Martial Arts franchise, working with us at Catch-Fire Funding to avoid any taxes or penalties in setting up their corporation. "My wife and I are real plotter types, so we took a leap." (It's paying off: in the first four months they'd already taken in fifty martial arts students.)

Pros of the Self-Directed 401(k)

APPROVE YOURSELF

You can skip the embarrassment of groveling in front of your banker for a loan and effectively approve yourself.

NO DEBT, TAXES, PENALTIES

With no interest to pay and no time schedule to repay the retirement funds, your business can enjoy improved cash flow without accruing debt and without taxation or other penalties.

MINIMAL PAPERWORK

Setting up a self-directed 401(k) plan requires far less paperwork than a loan application. A business plan and long application documents are not required to get self-directed 401(k) funding.

GET FUNDING FAST

On average, our clients receive their money from the rollover of their current retirement plan and purchase of their company stock in about three weeks.

OPEN-ENDED USE

You can use the money for salaries, equipment, inventory purchases, or any other legitimate business expenses, including a down payment on another loan.

QUALIFY FOR SBA LOAN

A self-directed 401(k) can help you qualify for an SBA loan, should you want or need one.

RETIREMENT PLANNING AND TAX DEFERRAL

A self-directed 401(k) can help you continue to save for retirement by allowing you to contribute a portion of your entrepreneurial salary back to the plan. The plan also allows for normal employer matching and profit-sharing contributions. Taxes on all of these contributions are deferred until the funds are withdrawn during retirement.

Cons of the Self-Directed 401(k)
RETIREMENT FUNDS MAY BE UNAVAILABLE

If you plan to continue your current employment, funds in your employer's retirement plan may not be eligible to be rolled out of that plan. Consult your current plan's summary plan description (SPD) to determine if the plan allows for what is known as "in-service distributions."

ASSOCIATED FEES

There are fees required to set up and maintain a self-directed 401(k). Your business-investment requirements and associated invested retirement funds should be greater than $30,000 to justify these costs.

REPORTING

Along with the normal management and tax-reporting activities required to run your business, additional time and effort will be required to successfully manage your self-directed 401(k) and comply with government reporting requirements. You can hire a 401(k) plan advisor to help you with these activities.

OTHER PEOPLE'S MONEY

While it's ideal to fund your new business with your own money, it is often not possible, so you may need to turn to other sources. There are several options, and you should weigh each one carefully so you can minimize debt and maximize cash flow in your business venture. Even today, in a postrecession era, banks can be very selective about whom they lend money to and for what purpose.

There are four typical types of loans. (A small-business funding advisor can help you procure any of them.)

SBA Loans

A Small Business Administration (SBA) loan is secured through a bank but backed (at least in part) by the federal government. From a bank's perspective, granting you an SBA loan is more favorable than a conventional loan because the bank is not on the line for the full amount—it shares the risk with the government.

SBA loans come with very strict guidelines. For example, say you're applying for a $150,000 loan. Before the SBA and the bank will hand over the money, they'll want to know that you have $150,000 in collateral for them to collect should you default on the loan. This collateral might consist of things like houses, cars, boats, and other big-ticket items. Establishing collateral is all part of a rigorous loan application that includes reviewing your credit and financial statements.

Pros of SBA Loans
REASONABLE TERMS
The term for an SBA loan is typically seven to ten years, with interest rates generally below 3 percent. These parameters provide your business ample time to establish itself and pay off the loan.

CAN'T GET A CONVENTIONAL LOAN
For those who don't have the means to self-fund but also don't qualify for a conventional loan, an SBA loan can be a saving grace. If it's your only option, well, at least you have one!

Cons of SBA Loans
PERSONAL ASSETS ON THE LINE
Since your available collateral has to match the loan amount, you will, more often than not, need to put a number of personal assets on the line. The looming threat of having your house or car taken away is undesirable, to say the least.

GRACE PERIOD IS SHORT
Should you default on your loan, the federal government isn't big on grace periods. Your personal assets may be taken away sooner than you might think.

CONSIDERABLE DOWN PAYMENT
The stringent SBA loan guidelines require not only a pledge of personal assets but also a hefty down payment—typically 30 percent of the loan—which may be out of reach for many people.

ONLY ONE UNIT AT A TIME

Say you're interested in purchasing more than one franchise unit (location or territory). With an SBA loan, regardless of what the loan amount covers, the money can only be applied to one unit at a time. If and when you decide to expand with another unit, you'd need to apply for a separate SBA loan.

DIFFICULT APPLICATION PROCESS

Andrew Caplinger says he's found applying for an SBA loan a time-consuming and difficult process that hasn't paid off most of the time. "I'd been denied five or six times," he says. He did qualify for an SBA loan to help finance his new business, but he wouldn't have if he wasn't also contributing self-directed 401(k) funds. "SBA ended up putting in about $20,000 more than my own funds," he says—not a heck of a lot for the work involved in procuring an SBA loan.

Conventional Loans

A conventional loan is not guaranteed or insured by the federal government. A conventional loan is an arrangement strictly between the borrower and the lender and is based solely on the borrower's credit and financial history. A conventional loan typically becomes an option when someone is overqualified for an SBA loan. (The Small Business Administration is meant to help entrepreneurs in need of assistance; therefore, if your assets or liquid cash exceed the value of your loan, you could be disqualified for an SBA loan.)

Collateral is usually not required to secure a conventional loan, because the bank already knows the person's net worth and thus exactly what it can recoup from an asset standpoint.

Pros of Conventional Loans
MORE FLEXIBILITY
Borrowers of conventional loans may not be subjected to the same scrutiny as those getting SBA loans. Conventional loans may be flexible about securing personal assets as collateral and may require a less substantial down payment.

MULTIPLE UNITS
Unlike with an SBA loan, a conventional loan does not limit your ability to open more than one location of a given business. If you plan to open three locations off the bat, and your business plan substantiates the loan amount you're after, so be it. Conventional loan use is not monitored in the same way SBA loan use is.

Cons of Conventional Loans
LESS ATTRACTIVE TERMS
When compared to an SBA loan, a conventional loan will typically have higher interest rates and the length of the loan (the payback window) will be shorter. If the window is relatively short, it may be set up like a balloon payment, and the loan will become subject to the whims of the market and current interest rates.

TOUGHER TO QUALIFY
Conventional loans are typically the most difficult to qualify for. Getting a conventional loan for a business with no track record can be extremely difficult. Remember, it's the bank's money on the line, with no government backing, and if the bank isn't convinced either that the business is a good investment or that your business skills are

strong enough to invest in, a conventional loan can be a tough path to pursue.

Unsecured Line of Credit

If you have good credit, a solid business plan, and don't need to borrow quite as much money as a typical SBA loan, an unsecured line of credit may be an option for you. In fact, a smaller line of credit is realistic until you've proven yourself by establishing positive business credit. At that point, you're likely to be approved for increased amounts of credit. Think of this like a credit card with increasing limits. This line of credit is not "secured" by (tied to) specific collateral.

Pros of an Unsecured Line of Credit
NO SBA RULES

Just as with a conventional loan, how you use an unsecured line of credit is not subject to the scrutiny an SBA loan is. There is also no pledge of personal assets, and a less substantial down payment is required.

Cons of an Unsecured Line of Credit
LIKE A CREDIT CARD

Just as people get into trouble with personal credit cards, they can get in over their heads with business credit. It's much easier to detach yourself from the numbers when all you have to do is swipe a card. If you do go over your limits, the fees and penalties can be steep.

Home Equity Loan

A home equity loan is just what it sounds like: a loan that enables you to use the equity in your home as collateral. Beyond having enough equity in your home to cover the desired loan amount, you'll also need good to excellent credit and a reasonable loan-to-value ratio.

A home equity loan almost feels like it should fall into the "your money" category; however, since you don't intend to sell your house to free up the money, a lender is needed to front the money to you while you remain in your home. (Therefore, it's really the bank's money, not yours.) Typically, a lender will lend up to 80 percent of the home's value. You can, of course, always borrow less than the amount you qualify for.

Pros of a Home Equity Loan
FAIRLY QUICK AND EASY
This kind of loan is fairly easy to qualify for because it's automatically secured against your home. The bank doesn't have to spend time chasing down and assessing other assets. For this reason, once you're approved for a home equity loan, you can access the money in less than a week—sometimes in as little as two days.

LOWER INTEREST
Home equity loan interest rates generally follow the interest rates of the housing market, which can be less than SBA-regulated interest rates.

GRACE PERIOD
Not that you ever want to plan on defaulting on a home equity, or any other type of, loan, but if you do, it's not the federal government that will be after you (as with an SBA-backed loan). Should you de-

fault on a home equity loan, your home will be subject to a typical foreclosure process, which could take anywhere from a few months to a few years.

Cons of a Home Equity Loan
GOVERNMENT FEE OFF THE TOP
When you access the equity in your home, the government will take its share off the top. The government charges a 2 or 3 percent fee, which is meant to counteract defaults.

YOU COULD LOSE YOUR HOUSE
Having the possibility of losing your home hanging over your head as you try to make your new business a success, can put additional strain and stress on you and your family.

YOU NEED TO BE EMPLOYED
Generally, in order to qualify for a home equity loan, you need to be employed at the time you apply. Since the bank will want to see proof of income, you should, if you can anticipate the need for a home equity loan, secure it while you're still employed.

Loans from Friends or Family
While borrowing money, or essentially taking out a loan, from friends or family may be an option in some cases, it's not always a preferable one. Sadly, money often complicates, and can even ruin, personal relationships. If you decide to go this route, it's a smart idea to have a lawyer draft up a formal loan agreement with a payment schedule— that way a third party is responsible for maintaining accountability.

Grants

Yet another way to utilize other people's money is to apply for a grant. Grant money is often associated with nonprofits, but there are places where for-profit grant money can be found: e.g., Uncle Sam, community-development corporations, state agencies, and corporate players. Check with SCORE (score.org) or your local Small Business Development Center (SBDC) for details.

Pros of Grants
IT'S FREE MONEY

If you apply for and are awarded a grant, congratulations! There's nothing wrong with using free money to your advantage.

Cons of Grants
TIMING

Grants are often based on current economic-development needs in the community. Sometimes, there is incentive to develop, and at other times there is not. Your chance at getting a grant will likely come down to serendipitous timing.

NO GUARANTEES

This is an obvious one. Whenever you're among of an untold number of people vying for the same thing, the outcome is impossible to predict. This makes financial planning for your small business extremely difficult.

A CAUTIONARY TALE
A Business Start-Up Saved by Self-Directed 401(k)

A good place to end this chapter on business funding is with a cautionary tale about an entrepreneur who learned the hard way how *not* to finance a small business but was able to correct his mistake in time to steer his venture off the rocks.

Dave Christianson, owner of the Frogurt shop in Santa Fe, learned the hard way how cash-flow woes can almost cripple a new business. He found that his start-up qualified for a grant, but his bank missed the deadline. So Dave took out both an SBA loan and the maximum amount allowed in a 401(k) loan.

Once he got his frozen yogurt shop up and running, he had $1,500 in monthly SBA loan payments and almost that much in monthly 401(k) loan payments. Every month, Dave watched a painful percentage of his profits go out the door, and then the off-season hit. (Santa Fe's tourism drops dramatically with the advent of colder weather.)

Dave needed a solution, and fast. In a business forum online, he first heard about the self-directed 401(k) as a way to tap into his retirement money without paying taxes or penalties or accruing debt. (Remember, he was paying off almost $3,000 a month in loans!) Further research brought Dave to CatchFire, and we helped advise him in reworking his business-funding structure.

He learned that a self-directed 401(k) would let him pay off his SBA loan and provide the working capital he needed to stay in business. Dave loved getting rid of debt, naturally, but he had also long disliked his other 401(k) options.

"I knew there was no way I wanted to keep that money in my 401(k) because I just don't feel good about the economy," says Dave, who lost nearly $65,000 in the stock market in 2008. But he had enough faith in himself and his business to know he could put his money to better use with a self-directed 401(k). "I still have my retirement fund that *I control*, rather than someone else."

For more information about business funding, go to yourbest boss.com/funding.

BUSINESS FUNDING CHECKLIST

❑ How you choose to fund your business will profoundly affect your success.

❑ Aim to invest about 40 percent of your overall net worth in funds: all personal assets minus all liabilities.

❑ A 401(k) loan is a very different (and less desirable) animal from the self-directed 401(k).

❑ The self-directed IRA and self-directed 401(k) are ways to avoid debt, taxes, or penalties when rolled over into your own corporation.

❑ Be careful borrowing money from friends or family; make sure the loan is documented in a legal agreement overseen by a third party.

❑ Putting your personal assets on the line can add a dimension of stress to an already anxious time.

CHAPTER 13

....

Gaining Traction: The First Six Months

Have you ever tried drinking from a fire hose? Try launching a new business—the experience is similar. In the first six months you're going to get a crash course in all the things you didn't even know you needed to know. You are likely to spend more time reacting to the new experiences that head your way than acting proactively. You'll encounter your fair share of bumps in the road, but this phase won't last long, and it's a tremendous learning experience.

Although it can be tough (and not typical) to turn a profit in the first six months, it is possible. Take Scott Fessenden and his business partner, who opened a Wahoo's Fish Taco franchise in Huntington Beach, California. Their business type was a great fit for the locale, and after being open for seven months, they had turned a profit each month and ranked among the top franchise locations in the country. The better your product or service fits with your geographic region's needs and wants, the faster you'll gain traction. Location. Location. Location. After it, timing is everything.

YOU'RE GOING TO NEED HELP

No matter what size or type of business you own, you're going to need help during the initial phase, even if it's only in the form of moral support. So put pride and any ideals of self-reliance aside! This help can come in various forms.

Help from Professional Advisors

Surround yourself with accredited, well-referenced professionals such as an accountant/CPA, a business attorney, a financial advisor, perhaps a business coach or peer business-owner group, and the like. Benefits from their help can include

- objective perspective into your business,

- real-world success stories to emulate,

- and confidence building.

Help from Employees

If you're following the Boss of a Few or Business of Many model, you'll have the help of employees—employees who can *make or break* your business. When hiring employees, you really have to think of them as team members—almost like the players on a basketball team. Each player has a specific role and unique talents. You don't want a bunch of the same personalities and skill sets. In this vital phase of your business, you can't afford to keep employees who aren't adding real value.

Help from the Community

During this phase, you should also seek help outside of the company, in your community. Make the effort to meet the owners of complementary businesses. In addition to gaining peer support, you could be planting seeds for referral sources and doing the same in return for them. Don't let the heavy workload of this early phase of entrepreneurship weaken your community relations; keep up with your circle of friends—you'll need the emotional outlet and support.

Help from Your Spouse

Even if your life partner is not your business partner, he or she can be an integral part of the success of your entrepreneurial venture. Social and community obligations need to be maintained, and when it comes to family responsibilities the heavy lifting may need to fall to your spouse, at least for a while. He or she can be your cheerleader, conflict broker, voice of reason, family manager, short-term breadwinner, fill-in employee, or all of the above!

Domestic Help

The first six months of a new business is the time to make your personal and home life as easy and stress-free as possible—so seriously consider outsourcing chores such as house cleaning, shopping, dog walking, and the like. You may also want to hire a personal assistant, just to make sure important appointments and tasks don't get overlooked during this crazy-busy phase.

KEEP THE CASH FLOWING

The ability to maintain positive cash flow (during any business phase) is critically important. Even if you're not yet turning a profit, you should have a positive cash flow if you've budgeted correctly.

Those "contingency dollars" you tucked away—that extra 10–20 percent—will come in very handy during this phase. They could be used to cover the costs of

- additional furniture or tenant improvements,

- downtime, in the case of an unforeseen injury,

- or staying afloat if your clients pay late and your receivables begin piling up.

REFRAMING FEAR

There is no point mincing words here: the first phase of your new business will challenge every part of you—intellectually, emotionally, and physically. Be prepared: keep your head down and your spirits up. Push through this hard time because, without a doubt, things will get better—much better—once you get through the first six months. And recognize that fear is natural; successful people manage their fear and turn it into motivation. One way they do it is by tackling obstacles and completing tasks one step at a time.

One Step at a Time

When I first bought a computer-repair company, I inherited a handful of employees and a preestablished protocol for how phones were answered, service techs dispatched, and jobs completed. In the first few weeks, I noticed inefficiencies and began asking myself, Why are we doing things this way? I started looking at ways to make our processes and tasks more efficient—and soon faced a rising tide of improvements, which I then needed to learn not to turn into a tsunami that would drag me under. (Perfectionism and impatience are enemies of the entrepreneur.)

If you bought a franchise, however, you'll face few (if any) inefficiencies, since a large part of what you're paying the franchisor for is a proven system of processes and operating procedures.

If you're starting a business from the ground up, all the processes will be brand new, and you can build them any way you wish. Make sure you get professional advice on subjects that are outside your domain of expertise—say, accounting, HR, and/or legal—and be prepared to tweak your processes during these early months of doing business. Strike early when it comes to weaning out inefficiencies.

EFFICIENCIES = PROFITABILITY

Dave and Dawn Petty—the Oklahoma couple who started a business serving the rodeo industry—discovered a way to increase efficiency (and the bottom line) in the first phase of their business. When they started out, the Pettys were renting a digital scoreboard to individual rodeos. But that required the couple to mount and remove the scoreboard (including a video tower) at every customer site—a time-consuming process that required a good deal of heavy lifting.

To speed up the process, and therefore be able to book more gigs, the Pettys decided to purchase a scoreboard that extends out of, and folds back into, a specialized trailer, requiring virtually no set-up or takedown time. It wasn't a cheap piece of equipment; they needed about $200,000 to pay for it, which they got by rolling over Dave's 401(k) funds. But it was worth the investment, as it took their business "to a new level," says Dave.

AUTOMATE OR DELEGATE

Just like Dave and Dawn removed themselves from the process of manually erecting and taking down their scoreboard, it's usually a good idea—regardless of what kind of business you own—to at least look at how you might remove yourself from being involved in every process. Your goal as the owner should be to rise above the minutiae of everyday operations and instead focus your efforts on the bigger picture (such as business development, marketing strategy, and long-term objectives).

So, how can you free yourself from the trap of micro-management? Two ways, primarily: automate and/or delegate.

1. **Automate:** Look into the types of software (including many free applications) that can take over processes you're doing manually.

2. **Delegate:** Hand off the task to someone else in your business, or if you are running a Company of One, consider hiring someone (offshore? contract? family or

trusted friend?) to do the task. The cost will more than likely be compensated by the extra time you'll have to focus on revenue-generating tasks.

Delegation is something Andrew Caplinger is thinking about more and more all the time. Although he is very strong operationally, from his years managing grocery chains, and he knows his seafood product very well, he admits he is "not great with people all the time." Hiring a people manager could be a good move for him. "I'm probably not as good a delegator as I could be," admits Andrew. "I'm wearing all the hats, even though they don't all necessarily fit me well."

"Wearing all the hats" is a common phenomenon among small business owners, but that doesn't make it the best practice. At the very least, you should lean on experts to help you do tasks that fall out of your comfort zone or skill set. For example, since financial management also falls to Andrew, he has a retired accountant helping to set him up on QuickBooks. "I know how to sell fish, but I am not an accountant," Andrew laughs. "I believe in learning stuff the right way, from the right people."

Let's look at the thinking that should go into evaluating the processes that make your business work. For example, let's say you sell a product online and therefore it's imperative that your company receives an accurate and timely order notification. Ask yourself the following:

- Are you the person being notified when an order comes in? If so, are you the best person for that role, or could you delegate it?

- What happens after order notification? Whom do you tell (and how are you communicating with that person) to begin the process of filling the order?

- How long does this step take? Could it be sped up—perhaps with automation (software) or by removing a person or step?

- How can you measure or track results, to see what's working when you make changes to improve efficiency?

- Which of your business peers could you talk to who may have gone through a similar process improvement?

THE CURE FOR FEELING OVERWHELMED

The "gaining traction" phase can feel overwhelming, but there are some tangible actions you can take to get you back on track:

1. Look back at your business plan and your unique selling proposition (USP). Are you still delivering on your promise to your customers?

2. Talk with some of your customers, privately, one on one. What makes them tick? What keeps them up at night? How is their experience with your business so far? Would they recommend you? Why or why not?

Active listening and *honest self-appraisal* are key to gaining real, useful traction in your new business. The first six months of running a business provide the ultimate on-the-job training!

GAINING TRACTION PHASE: FIRST SIX MONTHS CHECKLIST

❑ Remember that cash flow is king.

❑ Manage your fears; turn them into motivation.

❑ Train yourself to focus on one task at a time.

❑ Refer back to your USP and business plan if you feel lost or overwhelmed.

❑ Automate or delegate to create the best efficiencies.

❑ Make tough decisions early.

❑ Consider outsourcing tasks on the personal and home fronts.

CHAPTER 14

···

Acceleration: Six Months to Two Years

By this time you've gotten a feel for the road, and seen some dangerous curves, but you're becoming better prepared to react (or even be proactive) to avoid mistakes. While acceleration certainly does not mean switching to cruise control, it's an important step forward and a distinctly different phase from gaining traction.

From six months through the end of your second year is the stage where you should start to *scale* your business—i.e., increase labor, infrastructure, markets, etc.—and to modulate the speed of your growth. You're beginning to work on the all-important formula: optimal amount of business + right quality/quantity of resources + timing = maximum profitability.

The Olenicks are a good example of how this phase can put jet packs on a business. In 2009, the Lititz Pickle Company LLC was born in their home in Lititz, Pennsylvania. Within a year, the couple had to lease a seven-hundred-square-foot facility to keep up with demand by local stores and restaurants. Then came out-of-state customers. Within a couple of years, the Olenicks had outgrown that space too, and decided to expand into the retail and restaurant businesses as well as pickle manufacturing. They found a good deal in the town of Venango: a couple of small tracts of land and a seven-thousand-square-foot building that required a $100,000 renovation, not to mention some $75,000 in pickling equipment and other capital expenses for the pickle production space behind the storefront and café.

Despite all this acceleration, the Olenicks have accrued no business debt. "When we decided to pursue this full time, we looked into how to use the 401(k) package I'd accumulated during my career," says Mark. Those retirement funds, put into a C corporation with the help of CatchFire Funding, formed the bulk of the Olenicks' funding; the rest was personal savings. Oh yeah, and a lot of sweat equity— by the couple, their families, fellow church members, friends, and neighbors.

DIFFERENT SPEEDS AT DIFFERENT TIMES

Growth for growth's sake is not good. That may surprise you, so let's break it down: *How* and *when* you grow are paramount. You want to accelerate your business, but timing is everything (as in so much of life). Too much growth at the wrong time can end up causing you problems.

Andrew Caplinger has learned firsthand, from his start-up fish market, that growth improperly managed can do more harm than good. "We have so much business, *we're losing business*," he says. "People don't want to wait. For example, during Lent there's up to an hour-and-a-half wait at the counter!" Because the food preparation is all manual and done fresh on site, Andrew and his staff cannot keep up with demand.

So already, in the first two years of operation, he's looking at options for expansion—albeit reluctantly. So far Andrew has invested $50,000 from a self-directed 401(k), $68,000 from an SBA loan, and $40,000 from a loan from friends. "Any future expansion will require more debt, and I'm not happy about that," he says. However, when you're thinking of adding a thousand square feet to your sixteen-hundred-square-foot facility within the first year, it's best to do some growth management as soon as possible.

Andrew's situation illustrates how *unbalanced growth* can hinder your venture—by taking on new business without having enough resources to meet it. Fifty customers standing around in the fish market, impatiently clutching tickets, is obviously not an ideal situation for nurturing repeat business. Not to mention the employees who may be feeling overworked and frustrated at not being able to provide the level of customer service they wish they could.

ATTRACT GREAT HIRES

Hopefully, by this phase your business is generating a positive cash flow, enough to enable you to hire quality employees. But you know what else helps you to hire quality employees? Benefits—such as the ability to contribute to your company's 401(k) plan. An employee who is serious about planning and saving for his or her future often turns out to be an employee who is a huge asset to your business.

Of course, in addition to an employee-employer contributed 401(k) plan, benefits such as paid vacation, health care, and flexible schedules also attract the best employees. And great employees are always a good investment.

HOW TO REGULATE GROWTH

Another business limitation that can result from growth is having too many employees, so they are not working to their maximum capabilities. Rapid growth might also result from acquiring the wrong type of customers—that is, people who don't necessarily increase overall revenue proportionally. You always want the highest-value customers possible.

So, how do you regulate growth? First of all, refer back to your business plan, which should have outlined your optimum customer base, staffing plan, rate of growth per year, etc.

Another way to regulate growth is to control how much you spend on marketing to attract new business. Even if you have the resources to market aggressively, you also have to factor in outside issues, such as the economy, when choosing how to grow your customer base.

Daniel Knak, of Minnesota, bought the company R&B Contract Manufacturing in late 2010—in the middle of a recession—so he had to be creative with marketing and business development (increase and decrease resources accordingly). He made a point of first leveraging the company's *existing* customer base—with positive results. Then he turned up the marketing tap as the recession ended.

THINK AND ACT STRATEGICALLY

Growth can often be driven by innovative thinking. It helps to ask yourself questions such as: How can I get bigger at the lowest cost? Who in my community might I partner with for mutual benefits?

Julie Richter started her insurance agency in mid-2014, working by herself in a hundred-and-forty-square-foot office. After a few months, she'd found enough business for an insurance company that they paid her a large bonus—enough for her to add a full-time administrative assistant. At the same time, Julie moved into a two-thousand-square-foot office space—the entire second floor of a car dealership in town—because of a simpatico relationship with the business manager there. Jenni Kazinsky works at her family's dealership and as an insurance agent (independent contractor) for Julie's company. Any buyer of a new vehicle at the dealership has an on-site insurance agent! A strategic move that benefits both parties came as the result of Julie cultivating relationships where interests overlap.

REFINE YOUR BUSINESS

A good way to regulate growth is by balancing the amount of traffic, the number of people who convert to customers, and economics. These three points represent a cycle you want to continue to increase over time. Optimally, more traffic results in better conversion, leading to increased economics. The more money you have coming in, the more you can afford to funnel back into driving traffic.

This is where refinement comes in. If you are able to step back and look at this three-way balancing act objectively, you may be able to implement small tweaks that can make a big difference to your bottom line.

To grow CatchFire Funding, I spend a lot of time refining this aspect of the business; I am meticulous about improving my sales funnel. I continuously tweak my Google ad copy and landing pages— even branching out into social-media advertising to feed my funnel from another angle. All the while I am blogging and creating various downloadable assets, from white papers to books.

The trick, especially during this phase, is to never rest on your laurels. Always be thinking, What can I do next? Just make sure you're only tackling one thing at a time; otherwise it's very easy to get overwhelmed. If you're familiar with Perry Marshall's book *80/20 Sales and Marketing*, you will know to think of it this way: 20 percent of what you do will affect 80 percent of your business. Choose wisely where to focus your efforts. Don't spend time on $10 an hour jobs like running errands when you can spend time on the $100–$1,000 an hour jobs that will move your business forward.

ACCELERATION PHASE: SIX MONTHS TO TWO YEARS CHECKLIST

❑ Manage growth by balancing number of staff with market demand.

❑ Evaluate which customers help or which hinder your growth.

❑ Attract quality employees by offering a 401(k) plan and other benefits.

❑ Regulate volume of new business by increasing or throttling marketing spend.

❑ Spend a lot of time learning, and applying, tried-and-true marketing strategies.

CHAPTER 15

Full Speed: Two-Plus Years

I have personally reached the "full speed" phase with three different businesses, and all three have been drastically different experiences. At the two-year mark with my computer-repair-services company, I was just happy to still be in business. I felt I'd accomplished quite a bit in establishing my own systems and drastically improving upon the business that I had originally bought. I was making decent money and was ready to coast for a little while, or so I thought. I learned a lot about myself during that ownership experience; perhaps the most important thing I discovered was that I can't sit idle for long (a common characteristic among entrepreneurs). My mind continues to try to solve the next challenge at hand. I spent the next few years continuing to grow the business, until I got bored, sold it, and moved on.

Today, with CatchFire Funding in its eighth year of operation, I am far along in the "full speed" phase. Thinking back to when I crossed the two-year mark, I realize I felt like I had finally come into my own. I was proud of the system I'd built from scratch, and I certainly had very capable employees on board to help me optimally execute my strategies for growth.

But like any wise entrepreneur, despite several years of successful driving, I am not able to sleep at the wheel. I know things can change—they almost always do!

EVERYTHING CHANGES, SO BE READY

The only constant *is* change—in relationships, in life, and most definitely in business. You need to drive your company *according to the conditions*, most of which are out of your control.

Marketing Changes

The world of small business marketing, particularly online marketing, is forever evolving. Just when you think you have it figured out, something changes—a new Google algorithm, social media du jour, online PR best practices, etc. Every change requires creativity and versatility on your part. Consider outsourcing this area to experts, so you don't end up chasing every marketing flavor of the month.

Technology Changes

Think about how many times you've upgraded your cell phone or TV in the last five years. If your business relies on any form of technology—and you'd be hard-pressed to find one that doesn't—you need to stay abreast of how these things might affect your operations. Again, consider outsourcing tech work to experts.

Customers Change

While the need for quality customer service might remain consistent, the best way to reach customers changes. It often involves customer-service technology (like the popular Zendesk help software). As consumers' attention spans continue to shrink, your job is to learn to communicate with them more quickly and effectively.

Competitors Change

The competition is something that will always force your business to evolve. Either you adapt or you fall behind. In general, the more proactive you can be—i.e., getting *ahead* of the competition—the better off you'll be. That means you cannot afford to take your eyes off what they're up to—in marketing, events, customer wins, everything.

WHAT SHOULDN'T CHANGE? YOUR CONFIDENCE!

One of the most valuable characteristics an entrepreneur can have is confidence. Now that you've reached the "full speed" phase you should have confidence in what you've learned and achieved so far. As things continue to change, continue to apply that confidence to the next challenge you have to tackle.

FULL SPEED WITH A FRANCHISE

You may be thinking that the notion of evolving and refining your business doesn't apply if you're running a franchise business. This is only *somewhat* true. As a franchisee, you're responsible for executing the business operations the franchisor has laid out for you. But to excel, you need to stay on top of changes in your market, the competitive landscape, and consumer trends.

Most franchise systems have an advisory board—a group of franchisees that meets regularly to discuss opportunities to influence the future direction of the business. This is a great way to get involved and make yourself visible and get your voice heard.

If you own a franchise business and want to continue growing, there may be an opportunity to open a second location with a new territory. You may also want to diversify and look into owning a different type of franchise.

HOW FULL IS YOUR SPEED?

If you do have the desire to continue growing and branching out, the time to do it is while you are moving full speed ahead. It's easier to keep momentum—that's just physics! If you have total control over your business and how it does (or doesn't) grow, you need to ask yourself, How big do I really want to grow—by 10 percent, 50 percent, 100 percent?

Ten Percent Growth

Maintaining speed over time typically means growing by 10 percent or less each year. If this is your goal, your operations can remain pretty steady, with small tweaks and improvements.

As a monetary example, if you did $500,000 in sales last year, and this year your top-line revenue grew by 10 percent, your sales would be $550,000.

Fifty Percent Growth

If your goal is to grow by 50 percent or more, you're going to have to explore *other revenue streams*. You'll need to reengineer your business—by adding additional clients, products, or services—to see that kind of increase.

In this instance, your sales would go from $500,000 to $750,000.

One Hundred Percent Growth

What about 100 percent growth—going from $500,000 to $1 million or more? That's "brass ring" level—very difficult but not impossible. You'll have to essentially double everything you're doing at this point. Extreme growth can have drawbacks: when you attempt to scale up that much, many things can fall through the cracks, or you could discover inherent limitations in your business model.

And remember, *it takes money to make money*. Before you make any growth plans, you have to account for the time and money it takes to research, market, and support the improvements, such as hiring additional employees or getting additional space.

SOCK AWAY PRETAX MONEY

No matter what your current or future growth plans, one thing is for sure: you've got money coming in at this point. If you funded your business with a self-directed 401(k), you have the opportunity to sock away a great deal of pretax money.

And if you put in place a 401(k) match program, you can sock away even more. Does your spouse, or other family members, work with you? They can contribute as well. You can continue to *build value* in your business at the same time that you replenish whatever retirement funds you originally rolled over.

THIS IS NOT THE TIME TO UNDERESTIMATE YOURSELF

Many business owners will start to plateau during the "full speed" years—and that's fine if you're getting what you need from the business, both emotionally and financially.

When you really dig deep, you'll likely find that a lot has changed since you first started. What parts of the business have you most enjoyed? Was it building the business initially? Or maybe maintaining smooth, ongoing operations has been your strong suit. Understanding these strengths and preferences are key in determining what your future capabilities might be.

Do you already have your sights set on finding an exit, or are you open to seeing what might be around the next curve? An exit doesn't have to mean the end; it could mean you're just getting warmed up.

FULL SPEED: TWO-PLUS YEARS CHECKLIST

❑ This phase should be a chance for your employees to become more specialized in their roles.

❑ Continue to improve your operations, keeping the 80/20 rule in mind.

❑ Learn to adapt to changes in technology, your market, and the competition.

Full Speed: Two-Plus Years

❑ A self-directed 401(k) will allow you to sock away a significant amount of pretax money—and put it right back into your retirement.

❑ During this phase, think about your exit from the business, no matter how many years away that may be.

PART V
Where to Next, Boss?

. . . .

As for your next job title, how does "boss" sound? Pretty great, right? And an important part of being your own boss is knowing how much road your business has left to travel or at least how long you want to remain in the driver's seat. As counterintuitive as it may seem, a responsible entrepreneur enters a business venture with at least a rough idea of what his or her eventual exit strategy would look like.

As a midcareer entrepreneur, planning with the end in mind is that much easier because you're dealing with a more definitive time frame than your twentysomething counterparts. That said, there are a variety of advantageous "mature" exit strategies to explore.

CHAPTER 16

....

When and How to Exit

Knowing the right time to step away from a business is not the easiest thing. It's important to note that exiting certainly doesn't need to imply something negative. In reality, a smart business owner always plans for the exit, and there are more options than you might think.

At this stage, what it really comes down to is *your definition of retirement*. Given your position as a midcareer entrepreneur, you're much closer to retirement age than your younger entrepreneurial counterparts. Therefore, the reality of *when* to exit may be much more clearly defined for you.

If you're anxious to flip the script to a leisurely lifestyle full of nothing but travel and tee times, you'll want to start "downshifting" your business sooner.

Assuming you have a solvent, and therefore attractive, business, there are really two options for *how* you exit:

1. Pass ownership to a family member.

2. Sell the business to someone else (nonfamily).

PASSING OWNERSHIP TO A FAMILY MEMBER

Mixing blood with business can be tricky. Sadly, many family-owned company handoffs turn acrimonious. So be sure to take note that as much as you love your offspring and other family members, you still need to *think like a business person*. If you're considering this option, here are some suggestions:

- Consider starting your family member as an employee, to show them the ropes in a safe, controlled environment, with you still at the helm.

- Give the family member(s) stock options so that at a future date they can participate in a stock option when you sell.

- Succession and estate planning may be reasons to consider moving your business into a family trust. Consult with appropriate legal and financial advisors to better understand the benefits and limitations.

- Consider whether you will keep collecting profit from the business after you retire.

The next generation may even be the reason you get into entrepreneurship in the first place—as was the case with Jennifer Bohling and Brian Glazer, who bought a Jimmy John's franchise in Texas for their son/stepson, Justin, after visiting him where he worked as general manager of a Jimmy John's restaurant.

"We saw how well Justin was doing there," says Jennifer, adding that she was initially inspired to buy her son a franchise because the parents of someone she knew, in his late twenties, helped him buy his first couple of franchises, and now he has eight of them.

Jennifer admits, "If it wasn't for Justin, we probably wouldn't have taken that risk," but they liked the experience so much that after only three months of owning the Weatherford, Texas, franchise unit, they purchased a second franchise and penned a deal to buy another eight Jimmy John's units in the next decade.

Justin, twenty-six, is a managing owner of the business. He owns 5 percent of the stock of the first franchise, and will have a 20 percent stock option on the second location, says Jennifer, who continues at her full-time corporate job in telecommunications sales but longs to dedicate herself to helping her son run the franchises. Clearly, in the case of this family, the business will be handed on to Justin, who has earned his way into ownership.

Pros of Passing a Business to Family
Legacy
If you set out to own a business with the intention of passing the keys to the entrepreneurial kingdom to your offspring, you will meet your own benchmark of success if you choose the family route as an exit strategy.

Phased Exit

Typically, when family—especially a younger generation—is involved, there is an opportunity to pass along the business gradually while still enjoying the benefits of continued cash flow. While grooming your son or daughter to be CEO, you can still collect a paycheck, and even structure the business handoff to occur slowly over time.

Cons of Passing a Business to Family

Emotion Clouding the Deal

Just like you shouldn't hire Uncle Joe or Cousin Mary to work for you unless they are truly the right person for the job, you shouldn't choose to hand your business to family unless you can look at that decision, and see that it's a good one, with a clear, rational eye. Get professional advice—legal, financial, even from family business coaches—so you can be sure you're doing it right. Talk with family members well ahead of exit time, to make sure everyone is on the same page.

Multiple Family Members

What happens when multiple family members are involved in the business? If you're attempting to divide the business among more than one family member, internal battles may erupt and things may get messy quickly—especially if there is significant money at stake.

No Takers

What if it's your dream to pass on the family business to your child but his or her dream is to do something totally different? It happens, and to avoid crushing disappointment and family strife, it's best to have a plan B lined up—i.e., a buyer for your business.

SELLING THE BUSINESS TO NONFAMILY

If you intend to sell your business to retire, you need to start talking to your accountant and a business broker about it in the first couple of years. They can help advise you on how to minimize expenses so profits are maximized. After all, that's what buyers will be looking for.

When you're ready to retire, a business broker will shop your company around to potential buyers. There are two ways to sell your business:

1. *Stock sale:* You sell shares (as they relate to your retirement plan) to the new owner and the money goes back to your retirement plan.

2. *Asset sale:* Some buyers don't want to do stock sales; they prefer a straight asset sale. This is less than ideal for you because you'll have to pay corporate tax.

The stock sale may sound like a slam dunk, but not so fast. Be aware that if you sell stock, the new owner inherits liability. To compensate for that risk, you may need to incentivize the buyer by offering the stock at less than its dollar value.

THE FRANCHISE RESALE

If you own a franchise business, you likely have a predetermined exit date. (Franchise agreements typically last ten years.) If you want to sell off the business sooner, that is known as a "franchise resale."

When proposing a franchise resale, you should understand that it's not just a two-person transaction. You have to go through the franchisor's head office to formally transfer your franchise agreement to another person.

Oftentimes, the franchisor will assist you in finding a suitable new owner for your franchise—especially if you are looking to sell a prime territory that is highly sought after by prospective franchisees. Even if your franchise is not profitable and you wish to sell, the franchisor is still motivated to help you because they aren't receiving any royalties from your business and would rather have someone running the franchise who can turn a profit.

SELL TO MINIMIZE LOSSES

Selling a business to minimize losses is the worst-case scenario, but it needs to be mentioned. Should your business or franchise not work out, you have a couple of options to minimize your personal losses. There are typically two ways in which your business could be "underwater" at the time you sell:

The Business Was Never Profitable

If this is the case, the business is not sellable (much like a house that's underwater in a down market). Your best option is to sell off all assets, like equipment, furniture, computers, and maybe a customer mailing list.

You'll likely get out with just pennies on the dollar (e.g., you invested $100,000 and get $10,000 out), but that's better than having to sell off personal assets or, worse, having to declare bankruptcy.

The Business Didn't Make Enough Money

You may want out if between your business expenses and personal expenses, the business doesn't generate enough cash for your lifestyle. On paper—when you remove your salary—the business appears profitable, and therefore it's sellable.

WHAT IF YOU'RE NOT READY TO RETIRE?

I've never had a well-defined vision of what my retirement will look like. I don't particularly yearn to relax on the porch in a rocking chair, nor do I plan to adopt a set of hobbies. The only thing I do know is that I want to live *a life of purpose* for as long as I possibly can. Right now my business allows me to do just that.

That said, exiting a business does not mean you have to be done with it. There are full exits, as in selling the business outright, and there are a variety of partial-exit scenarios, where you remain involved but your role might change.

The Partial Exit

Here's a personal example. Right now I'm in my midfifties and eight years into running CatchFire Funding. I can actually see myself operating this business for quite some time—ten, fifteen, maybe even twenty more years. However, I'm not exactly sure what my role in the business will be in the future.

FIVE AND A HALF POSSIBLE SCENARIOS

1. If I look ahead ten years, I see a definite possibility that I'll still be involved day to day, dealing directly with my

clients. I greatly enjoy those interactions and, at least at this point, I see no real need to change that dynamic.

2. In a different scenario, ten years into the future I may get restless and want to create an offshoot of my business, going down the path of more dedicated business coaching for a few select clients. In this case, I would bring in a CEO to run the daily funding operations (while I'd still enjoy the cash flow).

3. Then there is the possibility that I could sell the funding part of the business to a third party, while I continue with the brand I've created, consulting with small business owners.

3½. Of course, there is always the possibility that one of my children will want to enter the family business. (I list this as only half of an option, because I feel it may just be wishful thinking on Dad's part.) If this is the case, either scenario 2 or 3 could work—my son or daughter could become CEO during a transition to ownership or take over and buy a portion of the company outright.

4. Or I might find myself saying, like Monty Python, "And now for something completely different." A business opportunity I'd never considered before could come along, causing me to decide to sell my company outright and pursue the new opportunity.

5. Then, I may just get tired—tired enough to decide to hang it all up (sell the company for a big profit, hope-

fully) and kick back with my wife, enjoying our full retirement together.

Think I've given this some thought? Yep, and with good reason.
From my point of view, the more you plan for all possible outcomes,
the less you leave to chance.

In life there are always unforeseen circumstances, some of which
might force you out of your business. While none of us can predict
health issues or natural disasters, we can attempt to plan for things
like economic change and shifting government regulations. Those issues don't happen overnight.

Furthermore, it should be pretty apparent if your business is rid-
ing the wave of a soon-to-pass fad or dependent on technology that
will become irrelevant within a few years. If the writing is on the
wall, figure out how to turn the tables so you and your business are
not at the mercy of those circumstances.

THIS IS YOUR CHANCE TO CASH IN

Regardless of how you've funded your business, when you sell it, you
hope for a nice return to make your nest egg grow.

But consider this: If you've funded with a self-directed 401(k),
you've been able to add to your assets all along. In effect, you've been
throwing gold pieces into the pot for years, all tax deferred. Once you
sell your business—especially if you can work out a stock sale—the
profit from your sale can stay in your retirement account, not subject
to corporate tax.

While you determine your ultimate destination or figure out

your next steps, that pot of money is all yours, to do with what you wish. If you decide to upshift, and transition to something bigger, better, or completely different, having that money available could make for a very smooth ride into the future!

EXIT PHASE CHECKLIST

❑ Think like a businessperson, not a relative, if thinking about handing off the company to a family member.

❑ A partial exit strategy is an option; retirement doesn't have to be "all or nothing."

❑ Franchise resale is possible should you not wish to cut short the length of your franchise agreement.

❑ A stock sale is more advantageous for you than an asset sale.

❑ Profit from the sale can stay in your retirement account, tax-free.

CHAPTER 17

The New American Dream

The old American dream—plenty of work and benefits for all—is gone. We can no longer depend on companies to provide us with long-term stability. Today we're often disposable units, replaceable by cheaper workers or not replaced at all in the case of automation or mergers/acquisitions. That's not personal—it's the fallout of the increasingly global, shareholder-driven reality of the marketplace.

We can either lament the passing of the "way we were," or we can get behind the *new* American dream and view it as a blessing. That's right—a blessing.

You see, corporate America never *did* offer us much control over our working lives. It decided when and where we worked. Our earnings didn't necessarily correspond to our efforts. And we didn't always have the freedom to pursue ideas that mattered to us. We had to do what our bosses said, when and how they said to do it.

As employees, we never had the freedom to look out for the best interests of ourselves and our families.

You've just read the stories of people who paid into the American dream for decades—and who only *now*, as entrepreneurs, have that freedom—the freedom that comes with financial independence, decision making, legacy building, and gaining complete control over your family's future.

The American ideals of initiative, hard work, and meritocracy are being exemplified every day by new entrepreneurial ventures.

If you want what these people want, and are willing to go to any sane and legal length to get it—you now have a blueprint for how to achieve that goal, a treasure map for the new American dream!

You're more entrepreneurially ready than you thought, and that much closer to making your dream job a reality. And, hey, who doesn't want their dream job? Especially if it offers benefits like these:

CONTROLLING YOUR SCHEDULE

Initially, you'll work longer hours as an entrepreneur. But if you organize your company right and fully train your employees, before long you'll be in charge of a well-oiled machine. Ultimately, you'll have full control of your own schedule, and you will love it.

A SECURE JOB

If you have ever been let go from a job, or feel on the edge of it, you know about that gnawing fear in the pit of your stomach. As an entrepreneur, you're your own boss, and you never have to worry about being let go again.

UNLIMITED INCOME

Honestly, this is one of the biggest reasons people go into business for themselves. Whether you want a cushy nest egg, the ability to buy whatever you want, to help your kids or grandkids, or to travel the world, entrepreneurship can be your golden ticket to financial success and fulfillment.

PRIDE

When you build a successful business, you have a great sense of accomplishment. You visualized it, you executed your plan, and now you can say, "I did it!" On the other hand, it's hard to feel that way when you do the same thing day in and day out for your employer, and you don't feel inspired anymore.

TELLING YOUR STORY

When people find out that you run your own business, they're intrigued. They want to know what it is you do, and how it's doing. You always have a tidbit to share, and it never gets boring. When people work for a corporation, a lot of times they don't have as much to share.

TAX PERKS

Business owners enjoy some nice tax advantages. They may be able to write off travel expenses, books, computers and other tools of the trade, car payments, phone bills, dining out, trade shows, networking events, and much more.

A LEGACY

If you work in fields such as advertising, medicine, computer programming, teaching, or retail, it's hard to imagine that you could pass your career to your spouse or children. On the other hand, if you own your own business, that's something that you can either sell, and funnel the proceeds to your estate, or pass directly to your loved ones.

MAKING A DIFFERENCE

Want to feed the poor or help underprivileged kids go to college? Want to donate to cancer research or help abused women and children? As a business owner, you control where your funds go, and you can use your company's profits to make a difference in the world.

JOB CREATION

When you own a business, it's like you have a whole new extended family. Knowing that you're creating jobs for people and helping them provide for their own families is a wonderful feeling.

SKILL DEVELOPMENT

When you go into business for yourself, you learn a *lot*. You have no choice but to pick up new skills. And everything you learn as an entrepreneur will spill over into your personal life. If you used to procrastinate, you'll likely have an easier time starting that DIY project at home or that exercise plan. You'll learn that you can commit to changes, and, in effect, that can make you a better spouse, parent, and friend.

I'll leave you with the story of Dave Young, of Jackson, Missouri, because, in many ways, it epitomizes the factors at play in midcareer entrepreneurship. Take it to heart, and look to your *own* needs and desires at this stage in your life.

IT'S A DOG'S LIFE (AND CAREER), AND IT COULDN'T BE BETTER

Dave Young has the same get-it-done attitude now that he had when he graduated from high school and went straight into the military, advancing, in a decade, as far as he could in submarine communications. After that, he spent fifteen years in corporate IT and software sales, perfecting the mundane Monday-morning business-travel routine, while managing up to sixty employees.

Still, in every new city Dave visited across the United States, he'd always check out the local kennels and dog hotels and think, Oh my goodness, there's money here! That's because Dave had been a dog person since childhood and, in the back of his mind and in his heart, was a true entrepreneur waiting to break out of his corporate skin.

"Before there was Cesar Millan, there was my father," he says. Dave Young Sr. had worked with animals in the Navy. "I have a family photo of us kids standing in a circle. Dad has a dog and a seal— each on a tricycle, going around and licking our faces." Dave grew up in Southern California, on a navy base, and in grade six moved to a small farm in Illinois with a menagerie of animals including, of course, many dogs. "My cousin started the family saying, 'When I die, I want to be a Dave Young dog,'" he laughs.

When Dave approached his midforties, he started crunching numbers to see what it might cost to get the land, build the kennels, buy the breeding dog pairs, and assemble the rest of what his dream business would need, but he could never seem to find the right time to strike out into entrepreneurship. He stuck to his sales job, which paid well and felt safe.

Then Dave's dad had to go into a nursing home. A couple of weeks later, Dave's mom had a stroke, and within months his father died. "The weekend Dad died, my brother [Steve] and I had a long talk," says Dave. "We had the same realization: Mom needs our help. That's when I learned that Steve had lost his job and was feeling down." Dave told his brother what he'd been dreaming and scheming of and asked if he wanted to join him. That's when everything changed.

Right from the start, Dave looked for a way fund his new venture with as little debt as possible. He found out about the self-directed 401(k) and thought, he says, "Wouldn't it be nice to put that into a business that will actually pay me more than my 401(k) would pay out on my retirement." Still, Dave treaded carefully. "There's lots of gotcha. I didn't want to get hosed by the tax guys." CatchFire Funding helped Dave to properly roll over his 401(k) into his own corporation, so he would avoid taxes or other penalties.

He took his entire 401(k), several hundred thousands of dollars, and invested it in his company, Crazy Y Holdings Inc.—an ironic name given how sensible Dave was about it all. "I'm afraid of loans— to me it's 'red money' that costs me more to pay it back. . . . That's a bit of contention with my brother," Dave laughs (Steve, forty, is a partner in, but not an owner of, Dave's business.)

Dave also put some of his personal savings into the business and the purchase of a twenty-acre property in the countryside outside of Jackson, Missouri, not far from his mother. Dave sold his house in the Chicago suburbs, and the day after he moved, he resigned from his job. "The company came back to me with several counteroffers; I admit they were very tempting," he says. But he held his ground and opened Sweet Pea Kennels.

In addition to being motivated by his parents' changing life circumstances, Dave had a push from the other end of the generation too—his own sons, all in their twenties. They helped move him from "Pondering to execution," he says. The youngest son teased Dave about when he would make a decision: "So, when you're eighty?" And his middle son now "gives all the love and care to the dogs," says Dave. Both of them have moved in with Dave to help with Sweet Pea Kennels, as has Steve. And their mother will come live with them too, when she needs the full-time care.

Steve has also started his own business, primarily in marketing and vacation rentals, and worked with us at CatchFire to set it up. He and Dave are closer than ever as fellow entrepreneurs. "We spend more time together now than we have in the last forty years," says

Dave. "We walk the grounds of the kennel with coffees in hand. . . . It's taught us to work together, to learn each other's styles."

The brothers, and Dave's sons, have converted a pole barn into a breeding barn and are in the process of constructing at least twenty-eight new kennel spaces, complete with in-floor heating. "Building this has been a lot of fun, spending time with my kids," says Dave. "My son jokes that I will work from sunup to sundown if I'm left to it."

Dave is only getting started with his new corporation: he's exploring other business opportunities, both related and otherwise. To start, he's planning to open a dog hotel in Cape Girardeau, Missouri, which will grow into a chain in St. Louis, Indianapolis, and Kansas City. And he's looking at buying a liquor store in the Jackson, Missouri, area. "It's all about diversification," says Dave, "especially in the puppy business, where you can fall out of favor quickly." He says this surrounded by a sea of golden retrievers, German shepherds, Dobermans, beagles, and border collies, and he couldn't be happier.

Using his retirement funds *now* is the best move he's made in a long time, Dave says. "I struggle with the whole idea of 'retirement.' The years sixty-five to eighty-five aren't your best ones—with health issues, you can't travel like you used to. I don't want to spend all my retirement money in those years."

Dave is glad he's invested in a business where he calls *all* the shots, where he gets to work with family, and where he can channel his passion toward personal financial gain and satisfaction with his life. "Good or bad, people will tell you that it's my passion that stands out," says Dave.

The New American Dream

His passion now serves *his* future, *his* family, *his* community, *his* lifestyle—not some uncaring employer. He's had enough of working for the wrong boss.

Dave is living the new American dream.

How about you?

EPILOGUE

Entrepreneurship on Steroids

If you're thinking, Okay, so what's next? you're ready to become an entrepreneur! And it might qualify you as a contender for "entrepreneurship on steroids."

Once you've poured your money, tears, and sweat equity into making your business a success, and you get to the point where it runs like the well-oiled machine you intended, with efficient employees and operations, and a trained management team in place, you can step back and observe what you've created, or you can get the itch to do it all again!

Success is contagious. If you've created a business that's successful and earning you a nice return, who's to say you can't *compound* those efforts and those rewards?

HOW TO BUILD AN EMPIRE: MULTIPLY OR DIVERSIFY

There are two basic ways to build an entrepreneurial empire: multiply your existing units of business or diversify your portfolio with various unrelated businesses. A third way is to do both.

Grow by Multiplication

Within the franchising model, it's easiest to grow your entrepreneurial empire via multiplication. And there are two basic ways to do it:

1. The master franchisee model

2. Multiunit franchising

Master Franchisee

The "master franchisee" option involves buying a large geographic region and then selling off smaller portions of that territory to subfranchisees. That model has been embraced by Michael Schaul, as master franchisee of Maid Right in Frisco, Texas.

Michael sells franchises to house cleaners in different parts of his Frisco territory. They sign a long-term agreement to provide Michael with their services as independent owners. And they're motivated to earn more based on their own efforts. "This really works to keep down turnover," says Michael.

Multiunit Franchising

One way to quickly build an entrepreneurial empire faster is to invest in multiple units of a franchise. This can be done up front, with your initial entrance into franchising, or later on as you get deeper into being a franchise owner. Let's look an example of each approach.

ADDING TO YOUR FRANCHISE

To help their son become a business owner, Jennifer Bohling and Brian Glazer originally intended to buy a single unit of the Jimmy John's restaurant franchise. But that unit did so well that within three months they'd bought a second location. Soon after that, the couple signed a development agreement to open eight to ten Jimmy John's franchises over the next decade. "We have some investors, and they like the great success we're having," says Jennifer. She explains that they like the franchise's formulas for success (e.g., "a location near a college is an A plus") and appreciate the "awesome systems and processes at Jimmy John's."

BUYING MULTIPLE UNITS

If you're engaged with a franchise system, it's highly likely that a multiunit expansion opportunity is available to you. If you've proven successful with one location, this tells a franchisor that you'll be able to replicate that success with another location. You can buy a unit or two, and when you're comfortable, open additional units largely *using cash flow generated by the first units.* Some debt may be incurred for the later units, but the bank will be much more likely to give loans when you have that kind of a business portfolio established.

A growing number of midcareer entrepreneurs are choosing the multiplication effect as a way to make bigger money sooner. That was the case with Max Steiner, fifty-seven, of Little Rock, Arkansas. After working for three decades as a project manager for a private mining company, Max took early retirement. He'd reached the head of his division and didn't see himself climbing any higher.

It was finally Max's turn to call the shots; the problem was, he didn't have any shots *to call*. Both of his kids were away at college, and his wife, Sandee, still worked part time as a Realtor. Max discovered lots of free time wasn't his end goal.

"I wasn't ready to do nothing," says Max. "Plus, it would have been a stretch, financially, to make it" on his fixed income for the rest of his life. Max knew it wasn't realistic to rely on the stock market, but he also knew that he didn't want to return to the days of hands-on operations.

"I wasn't looking for a full-time job for myself; I was looking for a business investment," says Max. Basically, he wanted a Company of One, so he'd have no employees, but he also wanted a scalable business so he wasn't limited in how much revenue he could generate.

Max was attracted to franchising, he says, because having a proven business plan would require less involvement operationally. Working with a franchise consultant, he looked at many options, from haircutting to karate classes. Among the franchise choices was a concept called Sola Salon Studios, whose business model is to lease salon space to individual hairdressers. That meant Max could essentially play landlord and, as long as the spaces were filled, just collect checks each month.

Exactly what Max had been looking for: no employees, no inventory, and no need to be there every day. However, the Sola Salon model required Max to purchase *three* franchise units up front. "The investment was considerably more than I was prepared for," he says.

"I thought, yeah, wow, it looks great—but I can't afford this!" Then he learned about the self-directed 401(k), which made it doable.

"I probably could've gotten a loan, but it's not what I wanted to do at this stage of my life. I didn't want to get tied down to a huge commitment that way," says Max. "And the thing about the 401(k) rollover is I'm investing in myself. . . . I have a hand in what happens."

Max completed the franchise "discovery process" with Sola Salon Studios and opened his first franchise in Little Rock in February of 2014. He opened his second location in North Little Rock—self-directing more of his 401(k) to finance it—and has plans to open his third.

Grow by Diversification

Diversification is another form of entrepreneurship on steroids, one wherein you have diverse revenue streams. This can be a sound approach for new entrepreneurs who are more risk adverse or who are entering higher-risk ventures, so they aren't putting "all their eggs in one basket."

There are two ways to diversify your business. One is to buy and operate many different types of businesses—that way you have a backup should one sector or line of business go soft. The other way to diversify is by having multiple related revenue streams within a single business.

Related Revenue Streams

Andrew Caplinger is a great example of an entrepreneur who has the vision to expand his core business in related directions—by looking at his customers' "pain points," as well as their yet-unfulfilled desires. Not only is he going gangbusters with his fish and seafood market-restaurant in Indianapolis, but Andrew has also diversified the revenue stream by adding cooking classes on site! He got the idea to add the one-day, forty-dollar-per-person classes (with guest chefs) from his time at culinary college.

But there is an additional business logic to cultivating the cooking-class revenue stream. Andrew's cooked-food business is overly busy—it can barely keep up with the demand—so he wants to drive more customers toward buying raw fish and seafood to take home and prepare themselves. "We see about a 30 percent boost to our retail sales on the day of the cooking class," he notes.

Caplinger's Fresh Catch Seafood Market has also invested in a eight-by-twenty-foot food trailer for big catering jobs in the Indianapolis area. Clearly, Andrew is embracing diversification via related revenue streams!

Adding Unrelated Businesses

The Olenicks are a good example of another way to build. Not content to stop with the pickle business, since their move to Venango, a depressed area of their home state, Pennsylvania, they have undertaken a bigger mission that includes business start-ups that have nothing to do with food. In the spring of 2015 they opened an outfitting company in Venango to serve the regional passions for river kayaking, canoeing, fishing, and hunting.

"We're hoping to create jobs, to help jump-start the town," Mark says of their new business. He adds, proudly, that they're starting this business for about $10,000, again without debt.

There's a lot more to be said about growing your entrepreneurial venture—but for now, you'll have to visit yourbestboss.com/steroids.

ADDITIONAL RESOURCES

NOTES FOR MY BUSINESS PLAN
My unique selling proposition (USP) is

to offer (product and/or service): _____

_____

to (target demographic): _____

_____

In the region of (geographic location): _____

_____

Resources close by include

    College campus: _____

_____

    High-value residential area(s): _____

_____

Additional Resources

Sporting or entertainment facility: _____

_____

Selling via the Internet

National: _____

_____

International (which countries): _____

_____

My main competitors are

1. _____

_____

_____

_____

_____

2. _____

_____

_____

_____

_____

Required location(s) (specify square footage)

Retail: _____

Production facility: _____

Office: _____

Food service: _____

Required number of employees

Full-time: _____

Part-time: _____

Additional Resources

Training

    For staff: _____

    For myself: _____

Required inventory: _____
_____
_____
_____
_____
_____
_____

Potential partnership(s): _____
_____
_____
_____
_____
_____
_____

Potential investor(s): _____
_____
_____
_____
_____
_____
_____

Additional Resources

Start-up Funds Available

    Personal savings: _____

    401(k): _____

    IRA: _____

    Family/friend loan: _____

    SBA loan: _____

    Home equity loan: _____

    Conventional loan(s): _____

    Unsecured line(s) of credit: _____

    Other: _____

    Approximate total of start-up funds: _____

Other notes: _____
_____
_____
_____
_____
_____
_____
_____

Additional Resources

RELEVANT READING
AND RESEARCH MATERIAL

WEBSITES

SBA.gov—for information about Small Business Administration loans

Score.org—a great resource to check for small business resources in your local area

Americassbdc.org—America's Small Business Development Center: look here to find your local office

Catchfirefunding.com

BOOKS

80/20 Sales and Marketing, Perry Marshall—a deep dive into an infallible marketing law; a must for anyone deciding how and where to spend marketing dollars

The E-Myth, Michael Gerber—dispels the myths surrounding starting your own business and shows how commonplace assumptions can get in your way

The Lean Startup, Eric Ries—a practical guide to doing more with less, supported by plenty of real-world entrepreneur examples

Built to Sell, John Warrillow—a quick read in story form that illustrates the importance of having an original product and a proven process; also demonstrates an excellent exit strategy

Work the System, Sam Carpenter—an intriguing guide to making more by working less, based on a modification of your fundamental perception of the world around you

TAKE THIS
MYTH-BUSTING QUIZ

TO BE A SUCCESSFUL ENTREPRENEUR . . .

1. *You have to get into debt.*

   ❑ True

   ❑ False

2. *You should have a business partner.*

   ❑ True

   ❑ False

3. *You have an advantage if you're older (midcareer).*

   ❑ True

   ❑ False

4. *You'll do better if you have an original idea for a business.*

   ❑ True

   ❑ False

5. *All you need is a few years.*

- ❑ True
- ❑ False

6. *You have to be born with entrepreneurial tendencies.*

- ❑ True
- ❑ False

7. *The corporate world prepares you well.*

- ❑ True
- ❑ False

8. *You need to follow the latest marketing system and tactics.*

- ❑ True
- ❑ False

9. *You need formal business training.*

- ❑ True
- ❑ False

Answers: upside down on bottom on this page.

9. F   8. F   7. T   6. F

5. T   4. F   3. T   2. F   1. F

THE FULL PICTURE OF
401(K) FUNDING

WHEN AND HOW YOU CAN BENEFIT FROM
ROLLING OVER YOUR RETIREMENT FUNDS

Your 401(k) or IRA funds can be used in your own business in the
following ways:

Prelaunch Phase

- Utilizing a self-directed 401(k) can save you from having to grovel in front of your banker for a conventional or SBA loan.

- A self-directed 401(k) gives you the ability to invest in your business using pretax dollars—you won't incur taxes, penalties, or interest.

- This means you can launch your business in the best possible position—debt-free and cash rich.

Gaining Traction Phase: First Six Months

- During this critical phase, you won't have to watch your profits go out the door in the form of monthly loan payments.

- Your retirement plan enables you to invest pretax dollars. Instead of paying taxes on that money, you're putting it away for retirement.

- As you hire employees, your 401(k) can be a huge benefit in helping you both attract and keep the highest quality help.

- When you set up a company 401(k) match plan, you're able to put away even more money (up to the maximum limits allowed by the IRS)—all tax deferred.

Acceleration Phase: Six Months to Two Years

When you get more comfortable with being a business owner, you can realize even more benefits of the self-directed 401(k). For example, your spouse, and even people outside your family, can invest in your business. There are two ways for them to do this:

1. If they will be working as employees of your company, they can roll their retirement funds into your new retirement plan.

2. Others can invest in your company's stock by purchasing it directly, without going through your self-directed 401(k) plan.

Full Speed Phase: Two-Plus Years

As you really get going with your business, keep this in mind: investing your retirement funds into your business gives you full control over the return on that investment—you're not at the mercy of the stock market or anyone else. The harder you work, the more successful and valuable your business is likely to become.

Who is going to work harder than you to grow your money?

Exit Phase

The ultimate way to pay yourself back is by building equity in your business, creating a valuable asset that you can sell for a profit when you're ready to exit.

Once you sell your business—especially if you can work out a stock sale—the profit from that sale can stay in your retirement account, not subject to corporate tax.

While you're determining your ultimate destination, or figuring out your next steps, your tax-deferred money will be *all yours* to do with what you wish. If you decide to upshift and transition to something bigger, better, or completely different, having that money available could make for a very smooth ride into the future.

ACKNOWLEDGMENTS

First and foremost, I want to thank my wife, my rock, my sounding board: Theresa. This book would never have happened if not for you planting the seed years ago and relentlessly fighting for what you knew the book could ultimately be. Our long drives with countless brainstorms and audio recordings became the all-important basis for the words within these pages.

My kids, sometimes in the most unexpected ways, have been a point of inspiration, not only throughout this journey, but at the heart of all my entrepreneurial ventures. The ability to set an example for my family is what gets me out of bed each morning.

I want to thank my parents for planting the seeds of entrepreneurship early on, instilling in me the values and foundation for a successful life. You've not only supported my professional endeavors but offered helping hands with family and business whenever needed.

Another source of inspiration has been the unwavering dedication of my CatchFire Funding staff. From their daily enthusiasm for

Acknowledgments

helping our clients to the fresh marketing ideas they share—it has all contributed to what this book has become. I consider this exceptional group of people my extended family.

To my clients: It is a privilege for me to watch from afar as you nurture and grow successful businesses. I continue to be inspired by your work, and my greatest satisfaction is to witness each individual fulfill his or her dreams.

To Perry Marshall, Bryan Todd, and their staff: Your encouragement over the years built my confidence to the point where I was finally ready to share my knowledge and experience in book form. Your strategic direction has been transformative for me, both personally and professionally.

To my fellow Roundtablers: I so greatly cherish the opportunity to share my challenges and successes with you and the truly priceless opportunity to see my business through your eyes. A piece of each of you has shaped my business and, ultimately, this book.

To Susan Baloun: The past few years of professional collaboration have been a pleasure. So many times I've trusted you to be my voice—and you've made me sound better than the real thing. The marketing and franchise expertise both you and Justin Baloun have brought to my business has been invaluable. And while the process of creating this book has tested both of us, I'm confident we finally got it right.

And finally to Heather Angus-Lee: Without a doubt, it was your framework and process that made this book a reality. I'm still in awe of your ability to polish the words and transform them into a very readable story—even if you did have to crack your whip a few times. In short, I could never thank you enough for your contribution.

ABOUT THE AUTHOR

As an author, serial entrepreneur, and business coach, Bill Seagraves knows how to turn business-ownership dreams into reality. With more than twenty years of experience as an entrepreneur and financial-funding expert, Bill has been the voice of reason leading thousands of aspiring small business owners to self-sufficient success.

Bill started his career in 1984 as a successful product development and sales manager. However, being an entrepreneur at heart, Bill left the corporate world and purchased a small business that provided information technology consulting and services to businesses, large and small. After eight years, he successfully transferred that business to one of his employees and moved on to cofound a company dedicated to providing 401(k) funding and other lending services.

After helping to establish that company, he decided to pursue a broader business vision that included funding and entrepreneur education, and in 2008 CatchFire Funding was born. Bill and his nimble team rapidly grew the company, beating the recession and becoming a market leader.

Today Bill continues to manage this growing staff of extraordinarily capable small business experts—many of whom have start-up business or franchise experience of their own. In addition to managing daily operations at CatchFire, Bill proves his masterful multitasking and leadership skills as a member of a private, international roundtable of highly successful entrepreneurs.

As a recognized expert in the field of small business funding and financing, Bill is regularly invited to share his insights as a speaker and panel presenter.

Having been dubbed the "midcareer entrepreneur expert," Bill plans to continuously broaden his entrepreneurial education resources.